# THE THORNY PARADISE

## WRITERS ON WRITING FOR CHILDREN

# THE THORNY PARADISE

WRITERS ON
WRITING FOR CHILDREN

EDITED BY EDWARD BLISHEN

KESTREL BOOKS

KESTREL BOOKS
Published by Penguin Books Ltd
Harmondsworth, Middlesex, England

This collection Copyright © 1975 by Edward Blishen

First published 1975

ISBN 0 7226 5463 4

Printed in Great Britain by
Ebenezer Baylis and Son Limited
The Trinity Press, Worcester, and London

# CONTENTS

# INTRODUCTION

IF this collection of essays were to be dedicated to anyone, it might be to Arnold Bennett. An unexpected figure, perhaps. But Bennett foresaw those shifts within literature that, in recent years, have transformed the character and status of writing for children: and he did so nearly half a century ago, when there can have been no obvious reason for doing anything of the kind. In one of his weekly reviews for the *Evening Standard*, he wrote:

I look forward to a change in children's books. Some writer will suddenly discover, what everybody else has always known, that of all realists children are the most un-compromising. That writer will have a fearful fight with publishers, who will assert that they alone know what children want; but in the end the writer will win, because in the end writers always do.

And this vision of Bennett's has, in essence, come true – even though it was not, as it turned out, a matter of a single writer leading the way. There were certainly pioneers: and one of them was Geoffrey Trease. In the essay with which this collection begins he looks back at the state of children's literature when he was a young writer, in the 1930s. Not only were there no critical standards, but few books for children had roots in reality of any kind – either everyday reality or the many realities of the imagination. They were written to formula: and the formula was stilted and prudish. 'Modern books for children', George Orwell wrote in 1936, discussing an experience as assistant in a bookshop, 'are rather horrible things, especially when you see them in the mass. Personally, I would sooner give a child a copy of Petronius Arbiter than *Peter Pan*, but even Barrie seems manly and wholesome compared with his later imitators.' If Geoffrey Trease is now able to say that 'the taboos and silences of a generation ago are gone' (and if there are grounds for guessing that Orwell would feel considerably more respectful among children's books of the 1970s), Mr Trease's own work is partly responsible for that change. But the advance of children's literature from its dismal pre-war condition is, in fact, the work of a whole group of writers: not as a conspiracy, but as a response to curious and wonderful convulsions in the literary, moral and social landscapes. It was, and continues to be, a complex business, and inevitably this book is concerned with it.

But the book was not designed as a history or analysis of that advance, or as a manifesto, or anything of the kind. In collecting it, I set out with the most cheerfully loose of aims. My invitation to contributors was to write whatever was in their minds about their work or about the general state of children's literature. This might seem runaway editorial permissiveness. But I had little fear that my essayists, obstinately individual, would merely echo one another. At the same time I was confident that, in the matter of certain vital general ideas, what they said would, as it were, *add up*. Each intent on his own business, they would turn out, here and there, to have made important patterns. And this they have certainly done.

How much hammering there is, for example, at that uninstructed view of writing for children that is still common – even among those who, using our clumsy categories, we must call adult writers.* An otherwise perfectly intelligent American novelist not long ago told me of his scorn for those who write for children – women, he said, giving to wearing appalling hats and chunky beads. I cannot, as it happens, think of more than one contributor to this book who ever wears a hat (and hers, if I understand the world of womanly headgear, have the same quality of mischievous fantasy as her books). All of them might be negatively described as people who eschew beads of any kind. Some of them, of course, are not even women. One thing these essays do is to launch an assault on this curious failure of insight and of simple observation within as well as outside the literary community. How can it be believed that to write for the young is a lightweight literary task, suitably carried out by comic figures? Either literature is a single enterprise, each branch of it as honourable and vital as any other, or there is something very wrong. I was not surprised, as essays arrived on my desk, to find that many of them mount – some by frontal attack, tart, wry, good-humoured or scornful, and others by implication – a powerful barrage by way of reply to that deeply unhealthy view of the children's writer. The reply has been offered, of course, by individuals on many single occasions in the recent past: here they fire off their guns together, and I do not see what the enemy can do but surrender.

That thoughtless notion of the inferiority of writing for children hangs, of course, on a similarly shallow theory of the inferiority of children. 'I do not really believe that children exist,' says Walter Hodges in these pages, 'except in the rather special sense of their comparative inexperience.' One way of defining the best modern writers for children is to say that they have been moved by a particular awareness of the impossibility of regarding children any longer as negligible human beings. The literature from which Arnold Bennett and George Orwell recoiled was founded on perfectly dreadful patronage of the young. Children were little innocents, according to some thin stereotype of innocence: and what

---

* If it comes to pioneers, Hugh Lofting ought to be mentioned. Finding that his publishers were advertising his books in their catalogue under the heading 'Juvenile', Lofting said he would permit this only if adult novels in the catalogue were listed under the heading 'Senile'.

was written for them was designed to fortify their unimportance and ignorance. Another of the large ideas that take shape as one reads these essays is that more and more children's writers see themselves as addressing another child altogether than that expurgated creature. He is a child who, within the limits of his inexperience (or more positively, of his growing experience) is . . . in essence, Bennett's young realist: no innocent to be sheltered and shielded, or fed with a special and foolish diet. And other ideas emerge that relate to this one; for example, that the writer is drawing upon the intuitions of the child still alive within himself. Fascinating, and important, all this: because one sees that, just as the new writing for children might well close a wasteful rift within literature itself, so it promises to revive and celebrate certain essential connections between the experience of the adult and that of the child. I don't think it excessive to say that, in several senses, it pioneers a new unity of literature.

And so to what, for some, will be the most startling idea of all: that it might be argued that writing for children grows stronger and bolder as writing for adults grows more . . . inward, marked by self-doubting intricacy. Here and there, in these essays, the idea appears as a belief that children's literature keeps faith with the element of story, the concern with large fundamental themes: so feeding important appetites that are not as dead as the characteristic adult fiction of our time would suggest. There is obviously room for much argument here: but the idea is very strong, plainly points to a real movement within literature itself, and is at the roots of much writing that cannot possibly be dismissed as merely nostalgic or anachronistic.

These are some of the general ideas that arise from this discussion of their trade by a score or so of writers. But the essays remain highly individual: and in making theoretical patterns out of themes and notions one ought not to forget the cry raised by Nina Bawden, who sees the children's writer as being peculiarly hemmed in by well-meaning intermediaries between him and his audience. And in fact, this is a book full of personal statements, of glimpses of individual writers at work, as much as it is a book which inevitably raises issues and maps out a changing territory.

I have arranged the contributions according to no very strong design: but I hope with some sense of sequence. On the whole, essays that concern themselves with general ideas come at the beginning: others, more personal, together with workshop essays – in which writers talk specifically about the way they set to work – come towards the end. At intervals, to underline the scope and variety of writing for children, I have placed essays that belong strictly neither to beginning nor end: as with Ian Serraillier's essay on the writing of poetry for children, or John Gordon's concentrated statement about the tensions and jealously guarded difficulties that make it possible for him to write at all.

About the performance of his team, an editor should perhaps be as dry and detached as possible – the merest announcer: but if I had to choose two assertions in these pages that seem to me most finely to sum up the work of the best children's writers today, one of them would be John Gordon's: 'The boundary between imagination and reality, and the boundary between being a child and being an adult, are border country, a passionate place in which to work.' To which I would add Joan Aiken's answer to those who dismiss writing for children as an unimportant activity engaged in by writers of a timid or retarded disposition. 'To be a children's writer,' she says, 'you need imagination, iconoclasm, a deep instinctive morality, a large vocabulary, a sense of humour and a powerful sense of pity and justice.' No more: no less.

# I

# THE REVOLUTION IN CHILDREN'S LITERATURE
## *Geoffrey Trease*

When I became a children's writer, nearly thirty-eight years ago, children's books were not considered worthy of critical discussion. And if we search the dusty attics to remind ourselves of what most such books were like in the early 1930s, that attitude becomes understandable. The classics were of course venerated and beyond criticism, but contemporary writers did not count. The typical schoolmaster's view was like that of the old cowboy who said, 'The only good Injun is a dead Injun.' The only good author was a dead one. Even today this criterion survives in some quarters – there is a guilty feeling that only the classics are worthwhile. More than once, in my own experience, a teacher has mentioned to her class that she knows me, and the commonest reaction has been an incredulous cry, 'What, is he still alive?'

This would have been my own reaction in 1920. The authors I most admired, I assumed to be dead – and dead, I now know, they certainly were: Henty since 1902, Stevenson and Ballantyne since 1894, Kingston since 1880. There must have been some more recent writers, someone must have produced all those exciting yarns about the 1914 war; indeed, if I dredge my memory I can still bring up a few names, Herbert Strang, Major Charles Gilson, and Percy F. Westerman. But you will find little or nothing about them in modern surveys of the adventure story. It really seems as though, after Henty's death, nothing memorable appeared in this field for a whole generation.

In other fields there were some outstanding contributions: too few admittedly, but individually notable. In 1920 Hugh Lofting began his *Doctor Dolittle* stories. The next year came Eleanor Farjeon's *Martin Pippin in the Apple Orchard*. 1922 brought the first of Richmal Crompton's *William* books. 1924 saw A. A. Milne's *When We Were Very Young*. But we look in vain for comparable adventure stories, historical or modern. The adventure-avid child had to make do with Henty and Ballantyne and the pedestrian imitators who simply transferred their formulae to the early twentieth century.

As a consequence, ideas and values became ossified. A new story in 1920 or 1930 tended to be a fossil in which one could trace the essential characteristics of one written in 1880 or 1890. Such books were produced to specification. It is easy to imagine the list of 'do's' and 'don'ts' hung above the author's desk.

The British must always win. One Englishman equals two Frenchmen equals four Germans equals any number of non-Europeans. A 'loyal native' is a man, dark of skin and doglike in devotion, who helps the British to govern his country. A 'treacherous native' is one who does not.

Similarly, in history, the common people subdivide into simple peasants, faithful retainers and howling mobs. The Cavaliers were 'A Good Thing'. So were the French aristocrats, except for their unfortunate handicap of not being English.

It was still accepted, in children's adventure stories if nowhere else, that war was glorious. One can almost hear the publisher advising his author. 'Any amount of violence and slaughter, my dear man – and the threat of diabolical torture is always popular. Only, on no account – on *no* account – any hint of affection between the sexes.'

This pitfall was easy to avoid. Books were labelled, as strictly as school lavatories, 'Books for Boys' or 'Books for Girls'. Girls *could* be introduced as characters into the boys' adventure story, but only as second-class citizens. They were allowed if they could climb, swim and ride well enough to keep up with the action, but they must not obstruct the plot with the frivolous interests natural to their sex. They might inspire the young hero's chivalry, but they had better not engage his other feelings.

Does it seem exaggerated, this picture of the situation forty or fifty years ago? Let me quote a personal experience.

In 1935 I suggested to the editor of the *Boys' Own Paper* an article on my experiences at a Young Pioneer camp in the Soviet Union. He seemed interested, but as we talked I detected a certain hesitation, a perceptible nervousness. I was not surprised. 'Here we go again,' I said to myself, 'political prejudice, however innocent the subject!' I was mistaken. He came at last to the point that was bothering him. 'There's just one thing,' he said, 'half these Young Pioneers were girls, weren't they? And camping with boys? Do you *have* to mention that?'

As to the jingoist values inherited from Victorian books, consider these lines from a story written in 1923:

'The white dog!' hissed the Arab leader, and his scimitar grated against my cutlass . . . Backwards and forwards we fought, at times stumbling against the prone bodies of the slain. But his keen weapon, glinting like a great half-moon, grew nearer and nearer to administering the Arab's favourite blow – a keen thrust near the collar-bone, and a cruel wrench, causing the blade to positively *rip* the victim's body from the collar-bone to the fifth rib. I saw the dark triumphant face of my antagonist, the curved beam of reflected light raised to strike, and like a flash I ducked, and striking upwards with my left hand, administered a thoroughly British uppercut. And, because an Oriental can never understand such a blow, he reeled back, a look of almost comical surprise on his face. Ere he could recover, I lunged out with my cutlass and stretched him dead upon the ground.

I must confess that this quotation comes not from a published book but from a story I wrote myself as a schoolboy of fourteen. But its ideas were clearly derived from the kind of juvenile literature prevalent in 1923, and it gives a not unfair picture of what was actually coming out at the time. Here are some shorter samples from stories published by the Oxford University Press:

He snatched up the battered chair and swung it round in a vicious semicircle, so that it struck the heads of all three in quick succession. 'Yellow, eh?' shouted the boss. Wasting no time, he pulled out his revolver and shot the man down.

And again: 'You're a disgrace to your own colour! You make me sick, you rotten swine!' And one more: 'The instant the first native burst from cover Frank opened fire, shooting with an accuracy born of long practice on game.'

In the story from which this last quotation is taken the Africans are frequently referred to as 'savages' and 'niggers'. All three quotations are from stories published not in the 1920s but the late 1940s. No wonder that George Orwell said of boys' fiction, actually *in* 1940, that it was 'sodden in the worst illusions of 1910'.

It was the realization of this, seven years earlier in 1933, that impelled me to enter this field of writing, myself. In this field alone, it seemed to me, the 1914 war had altered nothing. In all departments of adult litera- ture – the novel, the play, the poem – that First World War had been a mental and spiritual watershed. We had come over into a new country in which everything looked different. Only children's literature was unchanged.

Two reasons why it lacked the vitality of other forms lay in the economic conditions under which it was produced and in the absence of critical standards. Both discouraged artistic effort.

The typical juvenile book of those days was bought outright by the publishers for a flat and final payment. The author had thus no financial incentive to produce work that would stand the test of time and earn royalties years hence. The sooner it was out of print, the better for the author. To survive himself, he must write another and another and another. It did not matter if it was only the mixture as before.

Serious reviewing hardly existed. The purchaser was usually a parent or relative, or a head teacher choosing prizes. Publishers' catalogues often described their series as 'Reward Books'. Such books were selected partly for their pictures and – even more – for their sheer physical bulk. As family gifts they must make an impressive package on the breakfast table. At the prizegiving they must be clearly visible from the back of the hall. Juvenile publishing was still largely in the hands of firms who specialized in it, and they knew all the tricks of the trade to achieve the maximum visual effect at minimum cost. Out of curiosity, the other day, I compared the vital statistics of two of my early books which came out in the 1930s, one published by a general firm, one by a big company used to the marketing of juvenile literature. The two stories are of the same length, about 45 000 words. The one specially 'bulked' for the juvenile market is ninety-six pages longer and twice as thick. It weighs a pound and a quarter. The other weighs half a pound.

Miss Margaret Meek has written well about this era, what she calls 'the period of the Bumper Books, those swollen puffboard monstrosities . . . judged by their bulk', when 'the influence of the hack writer was at its height'. Miss Meek has underlined the dearth of serious criticism in the 1930s, when a book such as *Emil and the Detectives* could appear in English without its quality being noticed. I can endorse this from my own recollections of that time. I myself knew nothing of *Emil*. Nor did I know that in 1930 a man named Arthur Ransome had blazed a new trail with a book called *Swallows and Amazons*. My own first books came out in 1934, *Bows Against the Barons* and then *Comrades for the Charter*, books inspired – or should I say provoked? – by the sheer badness of the historical fiction then being offered to children. They got little notice. Being unconventional they were occasionally denounced, but they were reviewed hardly at all. There was no platform on which they could be discussed. Even George Orwell, for all his interest in the subject, did not hear of their existence until five years later.

Yet things *were* moving. With hindsight we can look back on the 1930s and see the first peeping shoots of the future harvest. In 1936 two important things happened. The Library Association established the Carnegie Medal to encourage better standards of writing and book-production for children. And a little magazine came into existence, *Junior Bookshelf*, carrying conscientious and critical reviews. Two years later, in 1938, the National Book Council – now the National Book League – issued the first list of recommended children's books ever produced in this country, entitled *Four to Fourteen*. It was compiled by a trained children's librarian, and it is significant that to catch such a rare creature, then almost unknown in Britain, they had to go to the famous public library at Toronto and ask Miss Kathleen Lines. And a happy day it was for our publishers and authors when they did.

What books had Miss Lines to choose from? Here and there among the hacks, good new authors *were* appearing. 1936, Noel Streatfeild with *Ballet Shoes*. 1937, Tolkien's *Hobbit*, Eve Garnett's *Family from One End Street*, Edward Ardizzone's *Little Tim*, and Kathleen Hale's *Orlando the Marmalade Cat*.

New fields of fiction were being explored. The family story, the career story, the holiday adventure set in everyday life – all can be traced back to this period. In my own field, the historical, Basil Blackwell started a new series called 'Tales of Action', aiming to combine the excitement children naturally demanded with a high standard of literary quality. The first contributors were L. A. G. Strong, Rex Warner and C. Day Lewis. This must have been about 1936 – I wrote a book for the series myself in 1938. I don't know whether my fellow contributors shared my views about the ideology of current children's fiction – I don't think that even Day Lewis, though he had flirted briefly with Communism at this date, showed any propagandist tendency in his story. One author of those days who, like me, was consciously in revolt against the established values was that prolific Marxist, Jack Lindsay. He wrote a story called *Rebels of the Goldfields*, based on the famous episode of the Eureka Stockade in 1854, and I believe that the Oxford University Press turned it down on political grounds. It was then published, as my own earliest books were, by Martin

Lawrence. By 1938, however, I had got the propagandist urge out of my system, and I was finding it possible to say what I wanted to say without instantly antagonizing an ordinary general publisher.

This, then, was the position when the war came in 1939. The revolution in children's literature had begun – quietly – but it had definitely begun. A few authors, a few publishers, a few booksellers, librarians, critics and teachers . . . Forward patrols were pushing out, gaining a little ground here and there, testing the strength of the entrenched opposition.

The six years of the Second World War did not have the fossilizing effect of the First World War.

Authors went on writing, even though many were in uniform – and if a cynic interjects, '*because* they were in uniform', this particular old warrior will take no umbrage. The services did provide many of us with a lot of subsidized spare time. I wrote one book myself in the orderly room of a battalion to which I was attached as education sergeant. The colonel had no high regard for education. He did not see it as an effective aid to the slaughtering of the enemy, and, zealous though I was to arrange discussions, gramophone recitals and classes for soft toy making, I was not allowed many hours of the men's time for such purposes. So, when not writing reports, I did the only thing that would keep my typewriter clacking. Undeterred by a somewhat hostile and suspicious Regimental Sergeant-Major, who breathed down my close-cropped neck every time he went stamping behind my chair, I wrote another adventure story for Basil Blackwell. I was very much tempted to include a dedication, 'To the Officer Commanding the 30th Warwickshires, without whose lack of co-operation this book could never have been written.'

Despite paper shortages and the blitz on publishers' warehouses, a fair flow of good new books was maintained. Mary Treadgold and Pamela Brown appeared in 1941, with, respectively, *We Couldn't Leave Dinah* and *The Swish of the Curtain*. 1945, the year of victory, gave us an extra cause for celebration: Mary Norton made her debut with *The Magic Bedknob*. Ironically, that was one of the two war years when the Carnegie Medal was withheld, owing to an alleged lack of suitable candidates.

The economy standards of wartime book-production put an end to artificial bulking. Children's books underwent a healthy slimming process. So, when controls relaxed in peacetime, the stage was set for the better-looking children's book we now take for granted. It helped, too, that juvenile publishing was no longer the monopoly of a few old-established houses. More of the great general publishers were finding it worth while to build up a children's list. There was money in children's books, thanks to the increasing expenditure on both public and school libraries. At the same time – and this was an infinitely regrettable coincidence – it was becoming less rewarding to write or publish the average adult novel. It is some consolation, though an incomplete one, that in the last twenty-five years more and more novelists have had to turn their talents to juvenile fiction in order to live.

The post-war publishers introduced more elegant standards of production – it did not occur to them that a children's book was a necessarily inferior article to be treated differently from other books – and the post-war authors similarly took the line that a children's book deserved to be paid for like any other. Royalty payments became much commoner. Outright purchase of copyright, a tradition with many reputable publishers before the war, became more and more of a discredited survival. It is now more than a decade ago that the children's writers in the Society of Authors formed their own sub-division inside that organization, calling themselves the Children's Writers Group. Our first task was to carry out a survey of the position and then a campaign to improve it. We pretty well stamped out the last vestiges of a practice which had long operated to depress both the author's standard of living and the quality of his work. Today, no children's author worth publishing is compelled to part with his copyright.

I feel strongly about this subject, and it has tempted me too far forward along my chronological path. Before leaving the wartime period I must mention two other developments.

One was the starting of Children's Book Weeks by the National Book League in co-operation with certain enlightened librarians. Besides exhibitions, there were talks by authors, whose appearance on the platform, whether impressive or disappointing, at least demonstrated to the boys and girls that it was possible to have written books and survived. I remember speaking at one such Book Week in Ealing just before I went overseas. It wasn't the first, but it was one of the earliest. These affairs played a useful part in stimulating children to explore books they might otherwise have left unopened.

A similar effect was achieved, in another way, by the BBC's dramatization of new children's books as radio serials. During the war, and for a decade afterwards, the much-lamented Children's Hour was run by dedicated and discriminating producers both in London and the Regions. Many a fine book, many a talented new author, was introduced to the juvenile public through their efforts. I do not think television has yet found – if indeed it has looked for – a comparable way (I mean, in power and degree) of presenting contemporary children's fiction to the young public of today.

By the end of the Second World War all the varied factors I have mentioned had built up slowly, like water behind a dam, and peace provided the conditions for a break-through. Perhaps that is too sudden a metaphor. It was a more gradual process – a crumbling, a seepage; the change did not happen overnight. Take, for example, the improvement of critical standards. It was not until 1949 that *The Times Literary Supplement* started its first special section for children's books, thereby introducing what is now an important regular event in the publishers' calendar.

There were still in those years far too many mediocre books about, 'new' books ostensibly, but still serving up the old recipes that had been stale in the 1920s. I used to stare despondently at the stacks of review copies in front of me. The twins, the secret passages, midnight in the dorm, the gay Cavaliers, the comic foreigners, the howling savages . . . I did not know then – I could not see as clearly as I do now – how much progress *had* been made. I managed to air my discontent in a BBC book programme – it was some time in 1947. I was allowed only seven minutes, but to get seven minutes to talk about children's books was in those days quite an achievement. And that broadcast, short though it was, had – for me, anyhow – important consequences.

The New Education Book Club had just been formed and was commissioning new work of educational interest. As a result of my broadcast, they invited me to write a column on current children's literature. I was rather taken aback. I had strong feelings, certainly, but they were *feelings* – instincts and prejudices rather than a coherent structure of argument and evidence. I remember saying, 'But I'm not sure there's a book in it – I've never done anything longer than a newspaper article about it.' 'Go on,' they said, and they gave me introductions to teachers and educationists, and suggested lines of inquiry I could explore. I began to accumulate more ideas of my own. I talked to librarians, I balanced myself on tiny chairs in junior libraries, skimming through handfuls of books. I wrote to some of the most popular authors, Enid Blyton, Malcolm Saville and Captain Johns. I said – only in more diplomatic language – 'Why, apart from the money, do you write for children? I propose to quote you verbatim unless you tell me not to.' They didn't, and I did – and some of their generously long answers were both amusing and informative – on occasions perhaps more than was intended.

By the time I had explored all these avenues and left no stone unturned – finding various unattractive things under some of the stones – my problem had changed. It was not whether I could get a book out of my material but how much of that material I could squeeze into my 50 000-word allowance. That was how my little survey, *Tales Out of School*, came into existence.

Nothing like it had been attempted in this country before. Other people, librarians mostly, had produced studies in America and elsewhere. In New Zealand, in 1946, Dorothy Neal White had made her admirable contribution entitled *About Books for Children*, but even she was better informed on American children's literature than English. Also in 1946 Roger Lancelyn Green had just published the first version of his *Tellers of Tales*, but that original version, unlike the one which superseded it twenty years later, was addressed not to adults but to the older children themselves. It was informative rather than critical, and it was backward-looking. Then there was Harvey Darton's monumental volume, *Children's Books in England* – equally backward-looking, as its sub-title indicated: *Five Centuries of Social Life*. I, on the other hand, was interested in the past only in so far as it influenced the present and the future. I was essentially subjective, controversial, nakedly open to the charge that I was an interested party.

I was fortunate, though. The tide was beginning to run my way. Other voices were being raised. Eleanor Graham had attacked the old type of family story. 'Are we still satisfied,' she asked, 'with the familiar pre-war formula for "a good modern story" – to get rid of the parents, divorce the children from home surroundings and influence, and, in an atmosphere of artificial freedom, to project them into a succession of thrilling adventures, very unlikely to occur in real life?'

Dorothy Neale White had just written, in her survey:

Children's literature has changed inwardly. It has broadened its range and increased its depth . . . [It] has been slowly maturing, as modern knowledge – political science, sociology, anthropology, economics – all impinged upon it. Some men and women will regret that children's literature is becoming more and more concerned with the facts of life, in both a political and biological sense, and there may be some cause for melancholy whenever the sweet swift dream of childhood is disturbed. I think, however, that children's literature has gained rather than lost by its new awareness of the world and the way it works.

Perhaps Mrs White had been over-optimistic about the progress made. Teachers used to ask me in those days, when I lectured to them – for children's literature was gradually becoming a subject for lectures – 'Why are there no modern stories with working-class settings? Nannies and ponies mean nothing to the children we teach.' Part of the revolution in children's literature over the past twenty years has been the appearance of working-class stories – Frederick Grice's *Bonny Pit Laddie*, Barbara Willard's *Eight for a Secret*, Elizabeth Stucley's *Magnolia Buildings*, and countless others.

I remember how, at a Children's Book Week in Cumberland in 1947, two schoolgirls came up to me and asked why there were no day-school stories about children like themselves. Out of that five-minute conversation came my own story, *No Boats on Bannermere*, and its four companion volumes – a total of 300 000 words, a project spread over nine years altogether, but all stemming from that brief encounter in a junior library.

But how those simple everyday stories upset some of the older critics! In one, I hinted ever so delicately that my schoolboy narrator was developing an interest in his sister's friend. Wilson Midgley, then editor of *John o' London's*, wrote to tell me how much he had enjoyed the book – but what a pity I had spoilt it at the finish. In the next volume I allowed my four teen-agers to consume, at the family Christmas dinner, a single glass each of white wine. This brought me another personal letter from an otherwise sympathetic editor, in this case the editor of a Nonconformist weekly. 'Did I think it right,' he demanded, 'to introduce children to the cocktail habit?'

It is a far cry from those days to the books of recent years. I don't know what these two editors would have said about a scene in Rosemary Sutcliff's *Mark of the Horse Lord*, published in 1965. The young gladiator hero makes a pass at the barmaid in a wineshop. 'Phaedrus leaned across the table, flung an arm round her shoulders, and kissed her loudly. She smelled of warm unwashed girl under the cheap scent . . .'

Miss Sutcliff came on the scene only in 1949 and Cynthia Harnett two years later. Today, I suppose, we have a dozen or so first-class historical storytellers. When I did my research for *Tales Out of School* I think it is fair to say that not one of these had appeared above the horizon.

It would be possible to look at many other categories of children's fiction and trace a similar revolution during the last two decades. For me the most impressive demonstration was when, in 1964, I was asked to produce a revised edition of my survey. In fifteen years things had changed so much that I had to rewrite completely one third of my book, and scarcely a single page could stand without modification.

Since then, progress has continued. Authors and books multiply. Higher standards have been encouraged by more informed criticism from specialists and wider interest from the public. Journals such as *Junior Bookshelf* and *The School Librarian* have been joined by Margery Fisher's *Growing Point*, Anne Wood's *Books for Your Children*, Nancy Chambers' *Signal*, and *Children's Literature in Education*, edited from St Luke's College, Exeter. There have been the Bodley Head Monographs, there is a lengthening bibliography on the subject. A good children's book can hardly escape notice now. One that breaks really new ground is certain of discussion. And that discussion is not confined to the columns of a specialist magazine, it can spill out into the public lecture-hall.

Where do we go from here? What further barriers need to be broken down, what gaps remain to be filled? I look around me. The taboos and silences of a generation ago are gone. We have stories for children and teen-agers about childbirth and widowhood, about the problems of adoption and illegitimacy. An American story (*Grover*, by Vera and Bill Cleaver) deals with a mother's suicide, from the standpoint of her eleven-year-old son. A review described it as 'most suitable perhaps for the nine- to eleven-year-olds'. Sometimes I feel that the author is now so free that he has nothing to do but write better and better books, if he can. But then nobody is so conservative as a revolutionary grown old, and perhaps my eyes have grown too dim to perceive the new objectives and the new challenges.

One possible problem – I don't yet know how serious it may prove for the children's writer – is the multi-racial society. Nobody today – I imagine – wishes to write stories with the prejudiced national attitudes and sometimes offensive phraseology accepted without comment when I was young. But the honest historical storyteller, in particular, can now – in the hypersensitive atmosphere of some areas today – find himself in a quandary. It is plain historical fact that in bygone centuries – to take but one example – the negro was kept in a subservient position in British and American society. His modern descendants may wish to forget this tragic part of their history, but history it *is*, and it should not be falsified or suppressed out of consideration, however sympathetic, for the hyper-sensitive. Publishers have told me that they must now 'tread warily' because of the pressure-groups. It will be a thousand pities if such publishers lose their nerve and it becomes impossible for English writers to write for English children about whole fields of English history because it contains facts that some people would prefer to forget.

This is one possible problem. There is also one of another kind. In our understandable desire to raise critical standards and achieve academic respectability there is a lurking risk that we shall produce books to please teachers and librarians more than the children themselves. We must never forget that, whatever the other valuable elements in a story, the single indispensable one is entertainment. Certainly, children's leisure-time reading is of immense educational importance. I believe that Oscar Wilde once observed, in one of his more serious moments, 'It is what you read when you don't have to that determines what you will be when you can't help it.' True. But how wise, too, was C. S. Lewis's warning against a too self-conscious and schematic approach to imaginative creation: 'I will not say that a good children's book could never be written by someone in the Ministry of Education. But I should lay very long odds against it.'

# 2

# WHY WRITE?
# WHY WRITE FOR CHILDREN?

*Catherine Storr*

I AM a compulsive writer. I suppose that before I'd learned to write without too much difficulty, I was a compulsive talker. This is borne out by my memory of hearing my parents say, 'Catherine never stops talking'. I think I went on talking too much until the awkwardness of adolescence overcame the habit. But before that I'd discovered writing; and though it didn't cure me immediately of talking too much, it did provide a new outlet for the need to communicate.

What I needed to communicate was feelings. We were a very buttoned-up family as far as the emotions were concerned. I don't remember ever doubting that my parents loved us, but they never said so in so many words. They also weren't at all physically demonstrative; you had to be in considerable distress before you got picked up and hugged. Kissing was something that you did before going to bed or saying good-bye for a longer period. This restraint didn't come naturally to me at all, and besides being told that I talked too much, I was also frequently told that I shouldn't ask for displays of affection. It was recognized in the family that Catherine was sentimental, and that this should be discouraged. Until I was ten these reprehensible feelings had to be repressed, or carefully monitored so that they didn't offend my parents' austere standards. I can remember attributing one particular enthusiasm to my doll, so that I wouldn't be held responsible for it. It was a marvellous day in the country and I was aching to say so to someone, but I knew if I did I'd be laughed at, so I said, 'Ruthy is feeling sentimental. She says, "How blue is the sky! How green in the grass!"' But even this ruse didn't work. I was laughed at again.

What happened when I was ten was that the door suddenly opened. I was lying in bed with the curtains undrawn and I saw a huge white moon looking at me through the branches of the aspen poplar tree which stood about forty feet away in the garden opposite my window. It must have been spring, I think, because the branches were bare. I got out of bed and wrote a poem to the moon with a blunt pencil on a sheet of manuscript music paper, which was all I could find. It was blank verse and until that moment I'd had no idea that I could write anything more ambitious than rhyming couplets. It was a very exciting moment. Probably all the more exciting because it was forbidden to wander about out of bed after eight o'clock. The next morning I read the poem through and was rather impressed by it. It was a great deal better than I'd have expected.

After this I don't remember very many single instances because I think I was writing all the time. I wrote poems, though I think that then, and certainly later, poetry was generally the sign of some sort of emotional crisis. But what I wrote mainly was stories. I'd known for a long time that stories were what I wanted to read or hear, and also that I could tell them myself. I used to bribe my younger brother to listen to them. I hate now to think what a bore I must have been. If he'd wanted to hear them he presumably wouldn't have needed bribing.

At first these stories were exactly what you'd expect; imitation fairy stories, stories of girls who were misunderstood at home, or who, their parents being conveniently disposed of beforehand, had exciting and improbable adventures. As I grew older I became slightly more sophisticated in my approach and tried my hand at what I hoped would be adult novels. The trouble about these was that, as my parents were always pointing out, I didn't know much about adult life at first hand. This was a difficulty which I tried to overcome by turning more and more to a sort of fantasy, in which bizarre events happened to ordinary people. One, of which I wrote at least five chapters, was an up-to-date version of the immaculate conception, but it shocked my mother so much that I lost faith in it and tore it up. I wish now I hadn't; it would be interesting if shaming to read it again. All this time, up to my early twenties, I was busily sending off stories and poems to magazine editors and publishers. Not one ever got accepted. I am not claiming to have been an unrecognized genius; what I was producing was exuberant but not very good. It was also very fragmented, a lot of short pieces written in all sorts of different styles. I was quite conscious that I hadn't found my own, and I was trying out other people's, which was probably right as practice, but doesn't make for convincing reading.

By the time I left University, I'd begun to get discouraged. I didn't mean to stop writing; but I felt despairing about ever getting anything published, and I thought I'd better make up my mind to find another means of livelihood. There were several reasons why I decided to try to take up medicine; one of the most important to me was that I thought that as a doctor I would get that experience of life which was wanted in my writing. So I became a medical student and went back to college to learn the science subjects which I'd never tackled before. And then an odd thing happened. Just before embarking on this alternative career I'd had a long holiday, during which I'd written a children's book based on a fantasy about my doll – the same Ruthy who had felt sentimental. As usual I sent it off to various publishers and, as usual, back it always came. When it reappeared for the tenth time, about six weeks after I'd gone back to school, so to speak, I couldn't be bothered to open the familiar parcel. It lay about for a week or so, and then, deciding I'd better find another name to send it to, I opened the brown paper and found a letter of acceptance inside. The manuscript had been returned because the publishers wanted a few alterations. It was one of the most exciting moments of my life.

This, then, was the beginning of my writing for children. I've often wondered since why I went on. It might seem likely, once I'd qualified as a doctor and gained some of the valuable real-life experience, that I'd switch to writing for adults. The answer lies in a variety of reasons, some respectable, some less so. First, it was obviously tempting to continue in the field in which I'd made a start. Second, by the time I was writing again, which was ten years later, I'd got children of my own to whom I was telling stories – and this time they didn't have to be bribed – and some of these stories seemed to me worth writing down. These I consider quite respectable reasons. The third, which is less so, is my own remaining childishness. For years I wouldn't admit this, although I knew I wrote my best books not for my children, but for myself. William Mayne, when asked once for whom he wrote his books, said, 'For the child I once was'; I'm sure this is true of many writers for children, but I think it is also true that one writes for the child one still is. Lastly, I've continued to write for the young, not only long after I should have ceased to be childish, but also after my children were grown up, because of my lasting need for the story form.

It is still perfectly O.K. to tell stories for children to read, but it isn't for adults. We're all at present culturally brainwashed into believing that really mature adults with any pretensions to intellectual interests don't read stories with pleasure. Stories may be allowed if the emphasis is on something apart from the narrative: that is, if the book is a thriller or science fiction, or of political or social significance. Apart from these exceptions there should be a minimum of plot, and it is generally considered pretty vulgar to arouse in the reader a curiosity to know what happens next. I say this with feeling, because I've published four adult novels and I've noticed that my intellectual friends, after reading them, say doubtfully, 'Of course they are very readable . . .'; and then, as a rule, no more. They know they are not paying me a compliment and they know that I know. It is the day of the anti-novel, and what is so easy to read can't be much good. Fortunately for me this attitude hasn't yet quite reached the children's book market, and I'm hoping it won't in my time.

Before leaving the question of why I write for children I'd like to make one more point. People often ask me whether I wrote the earlier children's books specifically for my own children, and they are surprised when I say, No, I didn't. But that answer isn't quite the whole truth. The first stories I wrote after I'd had children were stories I'd already told them. But after the first volume I realized that I must keep the telling and writing separate. If I wanted to write a story I mustn't tell it first. The effect of its having been told was to make the writing stilted, as if I felt I had to reproduce the tone of my own voice; and as I'm no actress, this made for monotony. It also lacked excitement. I knew, too well, exactly what was going to happen; and though this didn't matter so much in a short story, it would have been death to a longer book. I'd never have been able to conjure up the energy to finish it. In a way this separation of the two approaches to relating a story gave me greater freedom; I was able to tailor the told-by-word-of-mouth stories to the immediate interests or needs of one particular child, while when I was writing I could use or discard whatever material I chose. And often I used the experience or the daydream of one of the children as a part, or a starting-off point, of something that I wanted to write for myself. For instance, the heroine of *Marianne Dreams* took her name from a Swedish child who was my eldest daughter's best friend for a short time, and Marianne herself had many of that daughter's characteristics; Polly was my second daughter and she was frightened of wolves; she had an evil-minded wolf under her bed in the way that some of us have bears and others burglars. Lucy was remarkably like my youngest daughter, and she did long to be a boy. But

I wasn't writing any of those books just for any child but myself; even if I'm commissioned to write a book I can't do it unless I can use one of the ideas for a story which are already inside my head, because I write what I need to write, not what someone else needs; if that happens to fit in with what other people want or like, that is lucky for me, but it can't be the first consideration.

Having said this, I must immediately qualify the statement. Writing for my own needs is paramount in writing fiction; it is usually not so in journalism. Here, partly for financial reasons, one can't always behave in such an arbitrary fashion; one often has to write on a subject chosen by someone else. This can, however, still be exciting; one writes to discover what one thinks and feels; the difficulty arises when one's had a degree of success in writing about one subject and offers proliferate for more articles on almost exactly the same topic, so that the territory becomes too well known and the writing loses any sparkle it may once have had. This is partly why I really prefer writing fiction to anything else; there, even if – as I suspect is true – I never get away from the few themes which for some reason engage me, there is at least the possibility of presenting them in many different forms, and each, at the time, is felt by me to be something quite new.

It is simple to indicate the approaches I don't use when writing fiction, but much more difficult to describe what my own approaches are. This is because as a writer I rely enormously on the unconscious, and when talking about this it is dangerously easy to give the impression that there is an inexplicable mystique about the whole business, often expressed in terms which suggest that the writer sits in some sort of trance, while 'my characters take over – I have no idea what they are going to do or say . . .': or '. . . I don't invent my plots, they just happen, it's as if some invisible hand were guiding my pen . . .' I personally don't like the implication in this kind of description of writing that there is an external influence, whether it's divine inspiration at work or daemonic possession. Nor do I believe that a total surrender to the feeling – which I acknowledge – of being 'carried away' produces good work. I believe that, however rich the material and great the impetus given by the dynamic unconscious, there must always be the more objective attitude, the power to judge, evaluate and shape into coherence, provided by the conscious intelligence. If this is absent, as it sometimes is, either from choice or involuntarily, the result is chaotic, as can be observed in the creative works of the insane or that done under the influence of drugs. I wouldn't go so far as to say that it is worthless, it may be appealing and interesting; but it is not art, any more than dreams are.

Although I can't subscribe to the mystical attitude towards this way of writing, and although I think that there is a rational explanation of the manner in which it works and the feelings it evokes, and I'm quite prepared to theorize about it in general, I am reluctant to try to explore its mystery when it is actually happening to me. When I'm in the midst of it I want only to go on feeling it and to profit by it, and I'm fairly sure that if I stopped and tried to analyse the process I'd kill it – for that occasion – stone dead, but this is saying no more than I could say about digestion or sex; I have the equipment to understand both of these common happenings from the rational and scientific point of view, but that doesn't mean that I need always use it. I may be aware that I shall digest my food and make love better if I don't think about the lining of my stomach or my hormones too much at the time.

Let me give an example of what actually happens to me, and theorize on that experience.

The first thing is that I get hit by an idea. It may be the idea of a situation or of a character or of an incident. I find it exciting. I can't keep it out of my mind. It constantly invades my thoughts, it gets dressed up in different guises, it becomes an obsession. I'm infatuated by it. It is rather like falling in love at first sight; reason and suitability and common sense don't play a conspicuous part. At this stage I don't attempt to analyse, I simply go along with my feelings. I don't often start writing round one of these ideas immediately. Sometimes I'll try it out mentally in various different forms, telling myself possible beginnings of the narrative in which it's to be incorporated. I generally find myself doing this just before I'm going to sleep at night. Sometimes I don't even do this much; I store the theme like fuel, as a potential generator of energy for the future. The main theme of *Marianne Dreams*, for instance, I'd had for six years at least before I began to write the book. At first all I knew was that it was to be the story of a boy who discovered that he could direct the course of his dreams at night by what he had drawn the day before. I remember that I had a picture in my mind of him getting himself – by his drawing – into difficulties at the bottom of a pit or a cave, and of his then drawing the rope which was to be let down to save him. When I came to write the book, the boy turned into a girl, and the only similarity to that rescue from the pit is Mark's final departure by helicopter from the lighthouse, which is itself a place of refuge.

Judging from what happens when I feel ready to start writing, my unconscious has meanwhile been much more diligent. It's as if there was a part of it resembling a super-saturated solution of one of the salts, into which the idea has dropped like a crystal; immediately the solution itself begins to crystallize out round it, so that whatever pattern my conscious mind plans, both before or after I've started to write, must be conditioned by the design lying below the surface of my consciousness. It is this sense of a preformed shape, a sort of blue-print – not necessarily in full detail – which, I think, gives writers the feeling of being not wholly (consciously) responsible for their work. When I'm following the blue-print successfully I don't have to stop and consider as often as I do when I'm writing what is horribly called 'a think-piece', an article for a magazine, for instance, or an essay like this, for which I rely far more on a conscious intellectual process. There's a feeling of rightness, almost of inevitability, when everything is going well in my writing of fiction which is extraordinarily satisfying; but, by contrast, it is both frustrating and difficult to retrieve when it goes wrong, because all there is to go on is a feeling of having lost the way, and cerebration isn't as much help as a sort of blind searching for the sense of rightness and familiarity. There is also the practical side. It is extremely annoying to have to scrap several thousand words of reasonably convincing narrative and dialogue for no better reason than that it doesn't feel right. There is a passage in Nabokov's novel *The Defence*, describing the thoughts of the hero as he plays a vital chess tournament, and sees – or rather, hears, since Nabokov expresses himself here in terms of music – how any one move can determine the whole of the rest of the course of the game. This reminds me of the feeling I am trying to describe; it can resemble a striving after a harmony which, when one's achieved it, is approved as right by both the ear and the mind. Because, while this listening-feeling process is going on, the conscious mind must also be allowed its activity; it must be criticizing, judging, evaluating. If it isn't constantly ready to play its part, what is produced may be nothing more than an overflow of emotion, a purge perhaps for the writer, but not a communication which can reach other ears.

I'm not proposing, either here or anywhere else, not even to myself, to investigate why I'm attracted by any particular idea. That inquiry would be suitable for a psycho-analyst; and I'm content to believe that my choice is actuated by my needs, and that what I do with each idea may well be a sort of auto-psycho-therapy. It seems likely that each theme which appeals to me represents some unconscious problem on which I must do some work. A reasonably close analogy is that of the hungry man before whom is set a menu. Without going into the theory of dietetics or learning the physiological processes by which the food is broken down so as to provide what the body needs, he is perfectly capable of choosing his meal to fulfil his requirements. The body is fitted with excellent self-regulating mechanisms which instruct its owner to follow certain courses: to drink when he is short of fluids, to eat salt when he has lost more than he can afford, to avoid rich and fatty food when his liver is not functioning perfectly. In the same way, I can choose from the immense variety of day-to-day impressions what I need for psychological balance; whether I achieve it or not will, of course, depend on the accuracy of my original choice – and just as a diseased body will make erratic choices in physiological terms, so a diseased mind will occupy itself with bizarre subjects – and the skill with which I handle what I choose.

What else? The actual physical process of writing. I'm lucky, I can write anywhere and through surrounding activity and quite a lot of external noise. I used always to write everything by hand, but now I'm more used to it, I write on a typewriter by choice, and by hand only if using a machine is inconvenient. I've written sitting on grass, on sand, on rocks, on railway stations, in waiting rooms in airports. I like writing while moving; I write well on a train, better on a plane, best of all on a boat. I don't write in a disciplined way, so many words in a given period of time, nor always at the same time of day; I suppose you could say that whenever I'm not doing something else, I'm writing; it is both my job and my leisure activity. Like most other writers I find it difficult to start, easier to go on, particularly if I've broken off at a point which excites me; but even then I'm constantly on the look-out for some excuse to stop and do something else for a short time, preferably something that has an air of duty about it, like counting the laundry or writing a business letter. Deadlines are a help in resisting this temptation, and so, sometimes, is the excitement which can arise spontaneously when the mind has achieved just the right balance between knowing and unknowing, search and dis-covery. It's moments like this which make the business of writing worth while, and make up for the isolation and the disappointments. Not that I've ever worked out the advantages and disadvantages; because since I saw the moon that night when I was ten, I've never been conscious of choice. I feel like the Japanese Court Lady, Sei Shonagan, who wrote:

'And strangely enough to put down one's thought in a letter, even if one knows that it will probably never reach its destination, is an immense comfort. If writing did not exist, what terrible depressions we should suffer from!'

That was written well over eight centuries ago, but it's as true today as it was then.

# 3

# ON FIRM GROUND
## *John Gordon*

THERE is a white sheet hanging on the clothes line next door. It is a square of faceless space placed there, in the centre of the garden, against the trees. The darkness beneath the trees is pushed further back, tucked away within tunnels of branches so that the distant detail is as tiny and alluring as a scrap of faded handwriting.

Things are being said.

The sheet billows slightly, drifting across the lawn as though tugging and rocking with an invisible boat. The tip touches and then does not touch the corner of a shed. The edge of the sheet and the edge of the shed open to show the garden between them like the third leaf of a folding screen.

The handwriting, the boat and the screen exist in a suburban garden. Always there. The pleasure of story writing is to use them. The difficulty is to make them exist for other people.

For me writing is always an attempt to get to the edge of things, to reach that strangest of all places where one thing ends and another begins.

In order to do this it is necessary to stand on firm ground. Within a story there must be a reality that is all but touchable, a place in which things can happen. The starting point must be a place that already exists; we cannot free ourselves from what we know, and Mars is still landscaped on earth. A rigidity is necessary; imagination must be anchored. A story that attempts to dispense with rules is ink dropped into water.

Shape is a story's strength. A story is a shape. I have an ideal shape for a story; an image that can be drawn. It is the figure eight on its side. There is everything I want in that: equilibrium, pleasure (it reclines), and a focus of tension and a mystery at the exact centre. I would like to be able to write a story to that pattern.

So I begin a story with self-indulgence. The place is somewhere that is known to me and the story will attempt to please me by its pattern. But the instant pen touches paper there are other eyes looking over my shoulder. Even a diary, perhaps a diary most of all, assumes an audience, and those who say they write only for themselves are deluding themselves.

We all want to share our dreams. But we resist the dreams of others, and are as bored by an account of a dream as by being told the plot of a play. To engross others to the very limits of his own dream is the purpose of the story-teller. His self-indulgence is that it is his dream; the rest is discipline.

Writing for a young audience demands neither more discipline nor less than writing for anybody else. There can be no difference in standards; the only difference can be in boundaries, and they dissolve as they are approached. Every subject can be dealt with; it is only the technique used that indicates the audience.

The boundary between imagination and reality, and the boundary between being a child and being an adult are border country, a passionate place in which to work. Laws in that country are lifelines.

Until I discovered the necessity of restraints, writing was an impossibility. Now I am driven by a three-line whip: There must be a story, there must be clarity, there must be no boredom.

And the fourth is in the handwriting, the boat and the screen. On the coast the flat sea holds a straight line half way up the sky. Its near edge ripples uncertainly on the shore, like a sheet ruffled by an invisible hand that has the power to pull it back.

# 4

# A FREE GIFT

## Joan Aiken

THIS is not so much an essay as a rambling series of disjointed medita-
tions, and some questions without any answers, and some impracticable
suggestions.

To start with, a couple of quotations: their relevance will probably be
guessed. The first:

'Do you know where the wicked go after death?'
'They go to hell,' was my ready and orthodox answer.
'And should you like to fall into that pit and be burning there for ever?'
'No, Sir.'
'What must you do to avoid it?'
I deliberated for a moment; my answer, when it did come, was objectionable.
'I must keep in good health and not die.'
'How can you keep in good health? Children younger than you die daily . . .
Here is a book entitled *The Child's Guide*; read it with prayer, especially that part
containing an account of the awfully sudden death of Martha G—, a naughty
child addicted to falsehood and deceit' . . .
'I am not deceitful; if I were I should say I loved *you*; but I declare I do not love
you . . . I dislike you the worst of anybody in the world, and this book about the
liar, you may give it to your girl Georgiana, for it is she who tells lies . . .'

That, of course, is from *Jane Eyre*. And the other, quite different, is
shorter:

'Me and my brother were then the victims of his feury since which we have
suffered very much which leads us to the arrowing belief that we have received
some injury in our insides, especially as no marks of violence are visible externally.
I am screaming out loud all the time I write and so is my brother which takes off
my attention and I hope will excuse mistakes . . .'

I'll leave those for the moment in the air . . .

I keep my gramophone records in old wooden coalboxes. Quite by
chance I discovered a long time ago that old wooden coalboxes are exactly
the right shape and size for keeping gramophone records in. Don't worry

– there is a connection here: for someone who has been writing children's stories on and off for the last thirty years, the sudden rise to importance of children's literature has affected me rather as if I woke one day and found that university courses and seminars were being held on the necessity of keeping one's discs in old wooden coalboxes, and journals being printed called *Wooden Coalbox News*, and even an industry had sprung up for making imitation plastic wooden coalboxes . . . I don't wish to sound snide or ungrateful. In a way it's wonderful suddenly to find one's occupation so respectable, at least in certain company – for it isn't yet so with the general public. In most circles, the confession that one writes children's books always produces the same response, and very daunting it is. I was taken once to a party by friends. It was a very mixed party – all incomes, classes and professions, young and old: some guests were in television, some in films or advertising, some wrote. The only common factor was that they were all very intelligent, because the host was very intelligent. My friends started off by introducing me as their friend Joan who wrote children's books. But they soon stopped that. Because at the phrase *children's books* an expression of blank horror would close down on every face. People would be unable to think of a single conversational topic; they obviously expected me to start reciting poetry about fairies in a high, piping voice, and they couldn't wait to get away from that part of the room to somewhere safer and more interesting. Having observed this phenomenon, my friends changed their tactics – they began introducing me as somebody who wrote thrillers. Instantly all was well, and faces lit up – people love thriller-writers because everybody reads a thriller at one time or another. So they felt able to talk to me, and I had a good time and came away from the party with a curious feeling of the relativity of identity. And wondering, too, who is a real adult – if anybody is: all the time, that is to say.

Obviously, writing for children is regarded by society as a fairly childish occupation. But then it occurred to me that most people's occupations are pursued at a number of different levels – at varying mental ages. A man runs his business affairs with a fifty-year-old intelligence, conducts his marriage on a pattern formed when he was twenty, has hobbies suitable to a ten-year-old, and a reading age that stuck at Leslie Charteris. Is he an adult or not? And if he is not, how would you classify his reading-matter? There's a lot of what I'd classify as non-adult reading: thrillers, funny books, Regency romances, horror stories, westerns, for instance.

Of course, some of these, because of outstanding qualities, may fall into the adult sphere: but many don't. And yet it is considered perfectly all right for a forty-five-year-old company director to read, say, Ian Fleming, whereas he would be thought odd if he read, say, Alan Garner – a much better writer. And there is the same ambivalence in the social attitude to the writers. If you say you write books for children because you enjoy doing so, people instantly assume that you are retarded. Whereas, sad but true, if you say: 'Of course, I'd *rather* write adult fiction, but writing for children is more paying' (which, incidentally, is not so), people accept that as a perfectly logical, virtuous viewpoint. But to write children's books for pleasure – that, nine times out of ten, is considered almost as embarrassing as making one's money from the manufacture of contraceptives or nappy liners. And yet writing thrillers is all right. It's odd – because the really interesting point here is the strong similarity that in fact exists between thrillers and children's fiction; the moral outlook is the same: the pattern of mystery, danger, capture, escape, revenge, triumph of good over evil, is very similar indeed.

So society regards people who write for children as odd. And – if one does write for children – one can't help stopping from time to time and saying to oneself: 'Maybe society is right about this? Why do people write for children anyway? Is it a good thing that they should? Up to the nineteenth century, children managed all right without having books specially written for them; they were not regarded as a different species, but were clothed, fed, and treated in most ways as adults of a smaller size. Are they, in fact, better off for being treated as a separate minority? And, turning to the people who write for children, ought they to indulge themselves in this way? And what started them doing so, in the middle of the nineteenth century? Was it the need of the children, or the need of the writers to write in that particular way? And, if people are to be allowed to write for children, what ought they to write?'

I've started a lot of hares there, some of which I don't intend to pursue. The last question is particularly silly – almost as silly as saying: What ought people to write for adults? But I'd like to return to the first of my questions. Why do people write for children?

I'm afraid there are some – quite a number – who do it because it seems like easy money, especially in the recent boom in children's literature. Their idea is that in children's fiction you can get away with a minimum of factual background, a skimpy story, and a poverty-stricken vocabulary.

But let's set such people on one side. If they found an easier racket, they'd switch to it. Let's consider the ones who *like* to write for children. Let's consider why, in spite of its being an embarrassing, ill-paid, guilt-producing and socially unacceptable thing to do, quite a number of people in fact *do* it – instead of writing adult novels or plays or TV scripts or biographies, or as well as doing these things. What sort of people are they?

The answers to some of these questions may exist, and be available, in detail. For some years ago the Department of Motivational Studies in an American university set out to conduct a massive research project into the motivations of children's writers. They sent out a great questionnaire, which took a solid six hours to fill in, going at top speed: the results to be tabulated by computers. Though of course those results were bound to be an average only of the writers they selected – and who did the selecting, one wonders? I guess they'll have come up with such conclusions as that most children's writers are from broken families, and may have been ill when young, or handicapped, or misfits, or at least unsociably inclined. And I'm not sure where such a result would get us. We have left behind the era when boys were castrated so they'd always be sure of a part in opera; and you could hardly break up your home in the hope that your child might become a second Lewis Carroll. (It really is too bad that this project started too late for the questionnaire to be sent to *him*!)

However, let's – rather sketchily – survey a few peaks sticking up out of the general landscape of children's literature. We can agree that, yes, Dickens had a very unhappy childhood. (I include Dickens because, though not a children's writer, he has so many of the essential qualities of one: mystery, slapstick, simple emotion, intricate plots, marvellous language – and anyway, children enjoy him, and you could say that he wrote for a mental age of fifteen.) Kipling and Masefield were also unhappy as children. Beatrix Potter had tyrannical, dominating parents, and so did Charlotte Yonge. Ruskin and Lewis Carroll never entirely grew up. Hans Andersen's father died when he was small and his mother drank. Blake suffered from visions – and his being so gifted must in itself have made his childhood a troubled one. De la Mare was delicate, and so was Robert Louis Stevenson – who, moreover, had to endure a hellfire upbringing which caused him to have frightful nightmares and guilt fantasies. The theme certainly seems clear enough. Writers who had unhappy childhoods tend to address themselves to children: not necessarily all the time, not necessarily through their whole output – but, obviously, as a sort of compensation, to replace part of the childhood they lost, or to return to the happier periods which may have seemed particularly radiant in retrospect compared with the black times. They address themselves to children because they need to; they are writing for the unfulfilled part of themselves. It would be invidious to talk about living writers in this context; but I can think of a couple among the top rank who were ill when young or suffered from broken homes. It's interesting, though, that this seems to apply to male writers more than to females. Plenty of well-known female children's writers had stable, happy childhoods and led normal lives. Maybe women just take naturally to producing children's tales: it's an occupational occupation. They don't get such a complete break from childhood as men do, because they are more likely to be in continuous touch with children, one way or another, between youth and middle age. (This certainly happened in my own case.)

So we can guess that, as part of that American university's profile of the children's writer, there's a troubled childhood in the background. A probability that leads me to put yet another question, with the intention of causing argument: Is it a good thing that these disturbed, unhappy characters should be doing this particular job? Are the people who write for children the ones who *ought* to be doing so?

There are quite a few professions – for instance, politics, the police, the prison service, maybe the civil service – which, one suspects, attract the very last people who ought to be in them. The mere desire to be a prison warder or a prime minister should disbar one from eligibility. I dare say by the next century anybody expressing a wish to go into politics will be psychoanalysed and put through all kinds of vocational tests, as they ought to be before matrimony or being allowed to drive a car on the public roads. I know this is a shocking suggestion, verging on fascism: but we are moving into a more and more controlled way of living. Our environment has to be controlled: we are subject to restraints in many areas already – fluoridation, smokeless zones, no-parking areas, contraception, industrial regulations, the decision whether to die of nicotine cancer. Control isn't enjoyable – it's just necessary because there are so many of us. Some industries already have their own personnel selection tests; before taking an advertising job in which I wrote copy for Campbells' soup tin labels, I had to undergo a whole series of ability tests, and finally a psychologist spent two hours trying to make me lose my temper. If one needs such stringent tests in order to write advertising copy, the end-purposes of which may reasonably be regarded as frivolous, if not downright nefarious, then how much more necessary might it not be thought to subject to some kind of psychological screening those people who are directing their energies into such a frighteningly influential area as children's books? After all, they produce material that can affect the outlook of whole generations to an incalculable degree.

I know this is an outrageous suggestion. Who would give the tests? What would they consist of? Who would assess the results? The whole idea bristles with impossibilities, and certainly runs counter to the growing permissiveness in the adult field as to what can be written and published. I'm not making the suggestion quite seriously. But it's worth thinking around. Bear in mind that you need a licence to keep a dog: you need all kinds of official authority before you can adopt or foster a child or start a school or even run a playgroup. Yet any paranoid can write a children's book – the only direct control is the need to find a publisher, and that's not too difficult.

Wouldn't some control over the production of children's books be a good thing? I'll stick my neck out even further. The average child, I've heard, is estimated in the course of childhood to have time to read six hundred books. Judging from myself and my friends and children, the figure probably ought to be less, because children read books over and over again – which is a good thing: better to read *Tom Sawyer* four times than four second-rate stories. So, six hundred books or less. But the book industry is unlike nearly all other industries in one marked particular: its products never perish. So those six hundred books have already been written. Without a shadow of doubt, any children's librarian could produce a list of six hundred titles, including all the classics and plenty of good modern books: enough to last any child right through. So where is the need to write any more? Particularly since writing for children is such a suspect, self-indulgent, narcissistic activity.

I'll leave that question in the air, with the others, and continue to think about writers. Of course, a troubled childhood in the background isn't the only contributory factor, or the world would be stuffed with children's writers. Many people who suffer from childhood handicaps go on to become politicians or psychoanalysts or bank robbers. To be a writer you must have the potential; to be a children's writer, you need imagination, iconoclasm, a deep instinctive morality, a large vocabulary, a sense of humour, a powerful sense of pity and justice . . . In addition, the ideal writer for children – I for one feel this very strongly – should do something else most of the time. Writing for children ought not to be a full-time job. I want to underline that – it's perhaps the most important thing I have to say in this essay: *writing for children should not be a full-time job.* Another thing Dickens, Masefield, de la Mare, Lewis Carroll, Ruskin, Kipling, Hans Andersen, William Blake had in common – children's writing was a sideline with them. (If indeed they were really writing for children at any time?) They had plenty of other professional interests. And that meant, first, that their writing was enriched by their other activities, other knowledge and background. It had great depth. It meant, second, that they wrote, when they did write for children, purely for love. And that is the way children's writing should be done; it should not be done for any other reason. Think of those six hundred books again – what a tiny total it is! It's frightful to think that a single one of them should have been written primarily to earn an advance of £250 on a 5 per cent royalty rising to 12½ per cent – or to propagate some such idea as that it's a very enjoyable thing to be a student nurse. And while I'm at this point I might as well add that I don't think any kind of fringe activity connected with children's literature should be a full-time occupation – editing, reviewing, publishing, anything. Everyone connected with these professions ought to leave the children's field from time to time in order to get a different perspective. After all, children live in the world with the rest of us, they aren't a separate race. I'm uneasy about this cult of treating children as creatures utterly divorced from adult life. In a television series, *Family of Man*, which compared the social habits of different races, what struck me forcibly about the New Guinea tribesmen, the Himalayans, the Kalahari bushmen, the Chinese, was how very serene and well-adjusted their children seemed to be, because they had their established place in the adult world. And yet I'm ready to bet that not a single one of them had a children's book.

There's no need to point a moral here – and anyway, we can't reverse the course of civilization. So I'll go on to mention a danger that every children's writer is likely to encounter.

Most writers – most people – have at some point the idea for a good children's book. And maybe something fetches it out: an unresolved trauma from childhood to dispose of, or simply the circumstance of having children and telling them stories which seem worth writing down. In one way or another, this person, owing to some environmental factor,

writes a good book – maybe two or three. And then, although the for-
mative circumstances no longer exist, he or she is too caught up in the
business to quit. Financial pressure, pressure of success, pressure of habit–
it's easy to succumb. I can think of several people who wrote one or two
good children's books; and then their interests developed elsewhere in a
natural progression and they stopped. I can think of several more who
wrote one or two good children's books; and should have stopped there,
but didn't. And I need hardly say, since my previous remarks will have
made this opinion clear – but I will say it again because I feel so strongly
about it: Writing anything for children unless one has a strong, genuine
impulse not only to write but to write that one, particular thing – writing
anything without such an impulse is every bit as wicked as selling plastic
machine-gun toys, or candies containing addictive drugs, or watered-
down penicillin.

Another reason why children's writers should have some other,
predominant occupation is simply that children have a greater respect for
them if they do. Children, bless their good sound sense, are naturally suspicious of adults who devote themselves to nothing but children. For one
thing, such adults are too boringly familiar – there aren't any mysteries
about them. How, at school, we respected the teachers who disappeared
to their own pursuits when school was over! How we despised those who
were always at hand, doing things with the children as if they had nothing
else to do – no better way of occupying themselves! Elizabeth Jenkins, in
her book *Young Enthusiasts*, says: 'It is, of course, admirable to want to
teach children, but the question all too seldom asked is: What have you
got to teach them?' Parents, after all, are not exclusively occupied with
their children – or heaven help both parties! Surveys of distraught young
mothers in housing estates who never have a chance to get away show
what a very unnatural state of affairs this is, and how undesirable.

When I was a child, one of my greatest pleasures was listening to my
elder brother playing the piano. He was a lot older, and he played pretty
well. But the point was that he was playing for his benefit, and not for
mine. Part of my pleasure was the feeling that it was a free gift, that my
brother and I were independent of one another. Another part was the
understanding that some of the music was beyond my scope, which in-
tensified my enjoyment of the easier bits. If my brother had said, 'I'll play
for you now. Choose what you'd like,' I would have been not only em-
barrassed and nonplussed, but also horribly constricted by such a gesture:

it would have completely changed the whole experience. I think the essence of the very best children's literature is this understanding that it is a free gift – no, not a gift, but a treasure trove – tossed out casually from the richness of a much larger store. Of course, there are exceptions to such a generalization: I can think of several fine children's writers now at work who *at present* address themselves only to children. But my feeling is that they have the capacity to do something else – and will do so, in due course.

I listened once to a fascinating broadcast by Arthur Koestler. Its subject was literature and the law of diminishing returns, and Mr Koestler was discussing whether or not there is progress in art comparable with progress in science, where discoveries and the growth of knowledge can be continually recorded and tabulated. He came to the conclusion that there *is* progress in art, but of a different kind. It proceeds by leaps and bounds instead of in a measurable upward graph, and it skips from one form to another: each art-form proceeding through four stages. There's a stage of revolution, a stage of expansion, a stage of saturation – when the audience has had enough of it, and the only way their attention can be held is by exaggeration or involution – and then a final collapse, as something else comes to the fore. I suppose, judged in those terms, one could say that writing for children is just leaving its revolutionary stage, having been going for less than a hundred years, and is still expanding. Just now, because it is expanding, it attracts people who fifty years ago would have been writing novels. I wonder what will have happened in, say, another twenty years? Maybe involution will have set in, and there will be a kind of Kafka vogue in children's literature. I wouldn't be surprised at that – I believe one can see traces of it already. Anyway, I was thinking, after Koestler's talk, about this question of progress – that you can't have progress without loss. You acquire nylon, you lose the spinning-wheel. You acquire colour photography, you lose Breughel. You acquire logic, you lose fairy-tales. Our brains now have to contain such a frightening amount of *stuff*, just in order to carry on normal life: electronics, the decimal system, knowledge of what is happening all over the world, psychology, ecology, how to deal with parking meters and supermarkets and yellow tube tickets. When you think of all this information that has to be rammed in and stored at the front of our minds – compared, say, with the necessary equipment for comfortable and rational living at the beginning of the nineteenth century – you can see why some people worry about what in the meantime may be trickling away at the back and being irretrievably lost. Sherlock Holmes had an idea that the brain's capacity was strictly limited; when Dr Watson, rather scandalized, discovered that Holmes knew nothing about the solar system, and began explaining it to him, Holmes brushed his proffered instruction aside, saying: 'I managed very well before, without this information, and what you have told me I shall now do my best to forget.' I'm sure that, whether or not this idea of the mind's limited capacity is correct, many people entertain it; consciously or unconsciously it forms part of their fear of progress – the feeling that if you acquire enough basic data about space flight to be able to understand what is going on in the lunar module, you will probably forget your wife's birthday or the theme of the first movement of the third Brandenburg Concerto. I sometimes cheer myself up by remembering that in Peru they didn't learn about the wheel until bicycles were invented. I'm convinced that most children's writers are natural opponents of progress, unable to adapt to the world entirely, fighting a rearguard action, like people salvaging treasures in a bombardment. For growing up, of course, involves the severest loss of all, the one that is hardest to accept. Children's writers are natural conservatives in the sense that they want to *conserve*.

*

Let me go back to that question I asked, not very seriously: If people are to be allowed to write for children at all, what should they be allowed to write?

I hope it's a question that makes the reader's blood run cold. I'm glad to think that the notion of any restraints or controls over writers is a horrifying one. And yet on the other side of the Iron Curtain – for instance – such controls are in force. And in the field of children's literature, both in this country and America, I've come across educators who made fairly plain their feeling that some children's writers are a bunch of tiresome anarchists who could perfectly well be a bit more helpful if they chose, in the way of incorporating educational material and acceptable ethics into their writing. As if they were a kind of hot-drink vending machine, and you had only to press the right knob to produce an appropriately flavoured bit of nourishment! I need hardly say that I don't agree with this point of view. I don't think it's possible to exercise any control over what a creative artist produces, without the risk of wrecking the product. The only possible control is to shoot the artist.

This view may seem inconsistent with what I said before about who should be allowed to write for children. So it is. I don't pretend to have consistent views.

I wouldn't dream of making suggestions to other writers as to what they should write. But I do have strong opinions about the kind of intentions one should *not* have when setting out to write for children. Childhood is so desperately short, and becoming shorter all the time; children are reading adult novels at fourteen, which leaves only about nine years in which to get through those six hundred books – nearly two books a week. Furthermore, children have so little reading-time, compared with adults, and it's growing less. There's school, there's bedtime, and there are all the extracurricular activities they now have. I'm not decrying adventure playgrounds and drama groups and classes in clay-modelling and organized camp holidays . . . I think they are splendid: and even television has its points. But it all means a loss of reading time, and *that* means that when children do read, it really is a wicked shame if they waste any time at all on what I'll group together under the heading of Filboid Studge. That, you may recall, was the title of a short story by Saki, about a breakfast food so dull and tasteless that it sold extremely well because everybody believed it *must* be good for them. (Really it's a pity we don't have an excretory system for mental as well as physical waste matter. Children, at an age when their minds are as soft and impressionable as a newly tarred road, pick up such a mass of unnourishing stuff – and what happens to it? It soaks down into the subconscious and does no good there, or it lies around taking up room that could be used to better purpose.)

It's lucky that at least children have a strong natural resistance to phoney morality. They can see through the adult with some moral axe to grind almost before he opens his mouth. The smaller the child, the sharper the instinct. I suppose it's the same kind of ESP that one finds in animals – the telepathy that transmits to one's cat exactly which page of the Sunday paper one wishes to read, so that he can go and sit on it. Small children have this to a marked degree. You have only to say, 'Eat your nice spinach', for a negative reaction to be triggered off. You don't even have to add: 'Because it's good for you.' They pick that up out of the atmosphere. They sense at once when we want them to do something because it suits *us*. Sad to think how much at our mercy children are! Ninety per cent of their time we are organizing and guiding them and making them do things for utilitarian reasons – and then, for the remaining ten per cent, as likely as not, we are concocting pretexts for getting rid of them. I can remember the exact tone of my mother's voice as she invented some errand that would get me out from under the grown-ups' feet for half an hour. And I now remember too, with frightful guilt, how pleased I was when my children learned to read; apart from my real happiness at the thought of the pleasure that lay ahead of them, I looked forward to hours of peace and quiet.

On account of this tough natural resistance, I'm not bothered about hypocritical moral messages. That, as the reader will have guessed, is where the quotation from *Jane Eyre* comes in – the one I began this essay with. It's a beautiful example of the calm and ruthless logic with which children bypass any piece of moral teaching they are not going to concern themselves with.

> 'What must you do to avoid it [going to hell?]' . . .
> 'I must keep in good health and not die.'

It's an example of lateral thinking, anticipating Edward de Bono by 120 years.

Unfortunately, as children grow older, this faculty becomes blunted because of education. So much of education consists in having inexplicable things done at one for obscure reasons, that it's no wonder the victims presently almost cease to resist. I can see that some education is necessary— just as the wheel is necessary. We have to learn to get into gear with the rest of the world. But it's remarkable how little education one *can* get along with.

It's a dangerous thing to decry education. But I feel there is something wrong with our whole attitude to it. The trouble is that we have taken away the role of children in the adult world. Instead of being with their parents, learning how: helping on the farm, blowing the forge fire, making flint arrowheads with the grown-ups, as would be natural, they are all shoved off together into a corner. And what happens then? We have to find them something to do to keep them out of mischief. I think too much – far, far too much – of education is still fundamentally just this: something cooked up to keep children out of their parents' hair till they are grown. I don't see how you can learn to have a spontaneous, creative, intelligent, sensitive reaction to the world when for your first six or twelve or eighteen years there is so much of this element of hypocrisy in how you are treated. And the worst of it is that this element is present not only in education, but in reading matter too.

There's a whole range of it – from *The Awfully Sudden Death of Martha G—*, through *A Hundred and One Things to Do on a Wet Saturday and not Plague Daddy* – and *Sue Jones has a Super Time as Student Nurse* – to the novels (some of them quite good) intended to show teen-agers how to adjust to the colour problem and keep calm through parents' divorce and the death of poor Fido. My goodness, I even saw in a publisher's catalogue a series of situation books for *under-sixes*. I suppose they serve some purpose. But just the same I count them as Filboid Studge. And how insulting they are! Adults are not expected to buy books called *Mrs Sue Jones – Alcoholic's Wife,* or *A Hundred and One Ways to Lose Your Job and Keep Calm.* Maybe some adults would be better adjusted if they did. It's true people will swallow things wrapped in this form of fictional jam. They will swallow it because they have been conditioned to do so all their lives: because from the first primer their reading has become more impure. (I'm not using impure in the sense of obscene, but in the sense of being written with a concealed purpose.) In that same publisher's catalogue, advertising a series of basic vocabulary classics aimed at backward readers, the blurb said that in secondary schools a surprising number of children read nothing for pleasure except comics. Can you wonder at that, if the poor things have had nothing but situation books handed out to them? If you are bombarded with Filboid Studge, either you go on strike, or you become dulled and cease to recognize propaganda when you see or hear it. I'm sure if children's reading were kept unadulterated, they would be quicker and clearer-minded as adults, more confident in making judgements for themselves.

I can see an objection coming up here: some of the greatest and best-known children's books have a moral message. C. S. Lewis and George MacDonald: the Christian religion. Kipling: How to Maintain the British Empire. Arthur Ransome: How to get along without parents just the same as if they were there. They had a moral message mostly because they were rooted in the nineteenth century, when moral messages came naturally; everybody wore them like bustles. As we get farther and farther away from the nineteenth century, the moral message has become more cautious and oblique, though it is still often there. Don't mistake me—I'm not opposed to a moral if it is truly felt. You can't have life without opinions, you can't have behaviour without character. I just don't like tongue-in-cheek stuff. Konrad Lorenz said somewhere that our intuitive judgements of people are partly based on their linguistic habits. An interesting idea – I'm sure it's true. I certainly find it true in myself, and not only on an intuitive level: from someone who uses sloppy, second-hand phrases I'd expect sloppy, inconsiderate behaviour, whereas a person who uses vigorous, thoughtful, individual language will apply the same care to their behaviour – and this applies with double force to the written word. What I find myself meaning is that the author of a really well-written book needn't worry about inserting some synthetic moral message – the message will *be* there, embodied in the whole structure of the book.

Back to that other quotation with which I began – the quotation from Dickens: '"I am screaming out loud all the time I write and so is my brother which takes off my attention rather and I hope will excuse mistakes."'

The reason why I love that so much is because it's plain that it was written with extreme pleasure. You can feel his smile as the idea came to him and he wrote it down. You can feel this smile in plenty of children's masterpieces – in Jemima Puddleduck, and in James Reeves's poem *Cows* and in Jane Austen's youthful history of the kings and queens of England – to pick a few random examples. And there's a serious counterpart of the smile – a kind of intensity – you feel the author's awareness that he is putting down *exactly* what he intended – oh, for instance, in *The King of the Golden River*, and *A Cricket in Times Square*, and *Huckleberry Finn*, to pick some more at random. Really good writing should come out with the force of Niagara, it ought to be concentrated; it needs to have everything that's in adult writing squeezed into a smaller compass. I mean that both literally and metaphorically: in a form adapted to children's capacities, and at shorter length, because of this shortage of reading-time. But the emotional range ought to be the same, if not greater; children's emotions are just as powerful as those of adults, and more compressed, since children have less means of expressing themselves, and less capacity for self-analysis. The Victorians really had a point with all those deathbed scenes.

Some time ago I had a home-made picturebook sent me from a primary school in Cornwall: it was about Miss Slighcarp, the villainness in one of my books. Each of the children had drawn a picture of her and written on the back why they hated her. And then, under that, their teacher had evidently suggested that each should write down his own personal fear: 'In the kitchen, where the boiler is, the ventilator rattles and frightens me.' 'I hate Mrs Rance next door. Every time the ball goes in her garden she keeps it and I am frightened of her.' 'I am frightened of the teacher and my mum and dad when they are angry.' At first it was rather a worrying thought that my book had triggered off all this hate and fear, but then I thought – well, at least they are expressing their fears, and plainly they had an interesting time comparing their bogies and nightmares. Maybe it was really a good thing for them.

This is another thing a children's story ought to do, I suppose – put things in perspective; if you think about it, a story is the first step towards abstract thought. It is placing yourself on one side and looking at events from a distance: in psychological terms, mixing primary mental process – dream-imagery, wish-fulfilling fantasy – with secondary process – verbalization, adaptation to reality, logic. A story is like a roux – in cookery by the chemical process of rubbing fat into dry flour you can persuade it to mix with a liquid. So by means of a story you can combine dream with reality and make something nourishing. I think this mixing dream with reality, far from confusing children, helps them to define areas of both.

There's something I've said elsewhere that I'd like to repeat here: it's about the texture of children's books. Children read in a totally different way from adults. It's a newer activity for them – to begin with, they have to be wooed and kept involved. And then, when they are involved, reading for them isn't just a relaxation, something to be done after work. It's a real activity. (Children, after all, don't differentiate between work and non-work.) You see a child reading: he is standing on one leg, or squatting, or lying on his stomach – holding his breath, absolutely generating force. Children's reading-matter is going to be subjected to all sorts of strains and tensions, and it needs to be able to stand up to this at every point. Children read the same book over and over, or just make for the bits they like best, or read the book backwards. There's a psychological explanation for all this re-reading; apparently it fulfils a need for security, a need to make sure the story is still there. (Or you could just call it love, of course.) And children may read very slowly or very fast; they gulp down books or chew them, they believe passionately in the characters and identify with them, they really participate. In order to stand up to all this wear and tear, a book needs almost to be tested in a wind-tunnel before being launched. Furthermore, if it is going to be read and re-read, by the same child, over a span of perhaps ten years – my children certainly did this – then it needs to have something new to offer at each re-reading. It's impossible to predict what a child's mind will seize on at any stage. Their minds are like houses in a staggered process of building – some rooms complete with furniture, others just bare bricks and girders. Many children will miss humour in a story at first reading while they concentrate on the plot. Richness of language, symbolism, character – all these emerge at later readings. Conversely, anything poor or meretricious or cheap may be missed while attention is held by the excitement of the story, but sticks out like a sore thumb on a later reading. Reading aloud, of course, is the ultimate test – an absolutely basic one for a children's book. And I must add here that any adult who isn't willing to read aloud to its child for an hour a day doesn't deserve to *have* a child. I know this is probably an impossible ideal – both parents may be working, and there are so many counter-attractions and distractions – but just the same, there is nothing like reading aloud for enjoyment, and for building up a happy relationship between the participants.

Another factor which I think is of tremendous importance in this enrichment of texture is a sense of mystery and things left unexplained – references that are not followed up, incidents and behaviour that have to be puzzled over, language that is going to stretch the reader's mind and vocabulary. (Words, in themselves, are such a pleasure to children – and even the most deprived childhood can be well supplied with *them*.) Talking about mystery, I once came across a fascinating analysis of Wilkie Collins's *Moonstone*, in psychological terms, by Dr Charles Rycroft. He begins his essay by saying that people who have a compulsion to read detective novels do so as a kind of fantasy defence against incomprehensible infantile memories connected with their parents; they, as it were, keep on solving the problem over and over to their own satisfaction and pinning the guilt firmly on to somebody else. It's a very ingenious theory. I'm not sure that I agree with it altogether – I can think of plenty of reasons for reading thrillers – but I daresay that is one of the reasons why we all love a mystery.

As I've said, there's a very close connection between writing thrillers and writing for children – I know two or three people who, like myself, do both. And since, presumably, a wish to keep solving the unresolved problems of childhood, over and over again, characterizes the writer as well as the reader of detective fiction, then this ties in neatly with our image of the children's writer as someone with a troubled past.

As for children themselves – it's not surprising they are fascinated by mysteries. An immense proportion of the world they live in, after all, must be mysterious to them, since they are expected to take most adult behaviour on trust, without explanations. And not only adult behaviour, but anything else that adults themselves can't explain or haven't time to account for. And there's no doubt that children do love mysteries; they are poets, too; they have a natural affinity for the crazy logic of magic. And they like open endings that they can keep in mind and ponder.

Since children's reading needs richness and mystery, and a sense of intense pleasure, and dedication, and powerful emotion, and an intricate story, and fine language, and humour, it's plain that only one group of people are competent to write for children. They, of course, are poets – or at least people with the mental make-up of poets: writers who can condense experience and make it meaningful by the use of symbols. Not surprisingly, the best children's writers *are* poets – I wonder if the American university found that out!

I've said that I don't think children should be filled with Filboid Studge. And that the best children's writers should be mostly otherwise occupied, and should be poets. And I've ruminated a little about what should be written or not be written. But – except in so far as what I have said may have been a conscious summing-up of unconscious processes – I can't claim to practise what I preach. There is a relevant fairy-tale, which crops up in many folklores and so must carry a pretty basic message: the one about the helpful pixies. Mysterious little helpers do the farmwife's work for her every night – spin the flax, collect the eggs, make the butter, and so forth; but when she watches and discovers who is helping her and, to reward them, makes them all tiny suits of clothes, they put on the clothes, and they are pleased, to be sure, and dance all about: but that's the end of them. They disappear and never return. That tale is a powerful warning against too much tinkering with one's subterranean creative processes. I can't claim to write according to any of the lofty ideals I have put forward. But I said nobody should write for children unless they do it with their whole heart. And I can claim to do that.

# 5

# CHILDREN?
# WHAT CHILDREN?

## C. Walter Hodges

AMONG the defects of my character which by long practice I have learned to wear with complacency if not actually to enjoy, is an inability seriously to believe in the existence of quite ordinary phenomena which other people, less defective than I, expect me to receive with an astonishment equal to their own. For example, I find it hard to believe in the essential oddity or queerness of so many of my fellows. Their remarkable splendour, wickedness or beauty of soul, or whatever it might be, alas, does not impress me quite as it should, because (alas again) I do not believe in it quite as I should. Beauty of soul, to my disenchanted eye, is often apt to lose the top of its gloss on closer acquaintance, while wickedness can equally often produce such a stack of good excuses for itself, that in the end both the good and the bad, sitting down together, look very little different from any other two ordinary people sitting opposite me in a train. I tell myself repeatedly that in their off-the-train lives these everyday people are all very odd, different and peculiar. But in that case so also, probably, am I; and in *that* case, as Shakespeare said, the odds is gone, and there is nothing left remarkable beneath the visiting moon. Such a flatfooted attitude as this must label me a dull fellow, like someone unable to see a good joke when all around are laughing their heads off. To that extent I must regret it.

Paradoxically, however, it has some advantages; for where the odds is gone and everything is reduced to the ordinary, the ordinary itself tends to become somewhat odder than it was; and if I do not altogether believe in things that are staring me in the face, I may have a chance of finding something different behind their face-value, or at least of seeing them in a different light.

Take children, for example. I have never been able entirely to believe in children. Manifestly they do exist. They are everywhere to be seen, and may be recognized by certain special childish characteristics, such as their relative smallness, the occasional falling-out of their teeth, or their energetic and noisy running about, and so on. But as Bernard Shaw's heroine pointed out in *Pygmalion*, concerning the difference between Ladies and Flower Girls (back in those bad old days of class distinction when Ladies and Flower Girls were well understood to be very, very different sorts of people) the real difference was not how the Flower Girl spoke or behaved, but how she was treated. And the same is true of children. At different ages children are disadvantaged by their various degrees of merely technical insufficiency, such as not being able to read or write, or not knowing how to cast up a balance-sheet, or not being clean in their habits. But these are things which anyone can pick up, and most of us do, eventually. No, it is not for lack of these little skills, nor even because of their youth, but most often simply because they are *treated* as children, that children appear childish. Those who have had experience of bringing up children will agree, I am sure, that as regards their really important individual and personal characteristics, between infancy and maturity, the children they have known have not ever altered at all. I can speak from personal experience. I was myself a child for many years. I remember the condition well. Yet in all those years, although I can clearly recall being treated as a child, I cannot remember ever *feeling* like one, and I know for certain that, for better or worse, the essence of my emotions, tastes and aptitudes has not ever changed.

They are no different now from what they were when at the age of ten or thereabouts, being at that time a boarder wretchedly imprisoned in a small preparatory school, I spent a week's pocket money on an exercise book of cream-laid paper. Our weekly shopping was done for us boarders by the matron, a nice white-haired lady called Miss Brand, and I remember being very particular in my instruction to her about the cream-laid paper, which I felt to be a very superior quality for writing on, an instruction which Miss Brand faithfully carried out. Thereupon, in this exercise book, fat with cream-laid paper, I wrote my Opus One, a work entitled *Walks in Our Museums*. As I remember it, it followed rather repetitiously my own adventures after going to sleep in various interesting places such as the Egyptian Galleries of the British Museum or the armoury of the Tower of London, places which I loved then as now, and waking to find myself Back There, confronted by the Pharaoh Rameses II himself, who was drinking *Heqt* (the ancient Egyptian word for beer, an informational tit-bit much treasured by me at the time); or in the latter case by the headsman and the rack, with some diversionary time in hand for me to show off about the anatomy of plate-armour; for in those days I considered myself a dab-hand with armets, pauldrons, vambraces and the like.

The point of all this lush reminiscence is simply to illustrate the fact that I am here and now the same person who wrote of those *Walks in Our Museums*, and I might easily write the same book tomorrow, allowing only that I have since had time to acquire a greater degree of sophistication, and experience in comparative taste; as, for instance, that I would not now use that title, which I know to be a little dated and dull. I might call it 'The Museum Without Walls' or 'Remembrance of Things Past' ... But no, as I recall it, both these titles have already been taken up. Let me see, then ... well, it will not come at once. It will take a bit of time to get the title right. Experience has taught me to be fairly discriminating in this matter. It has also taught me certain techniques, such as the productive use of simple patience. I know now from experience that the 'right' title will come to me by itself in due course, from a sort of subconscious process of gestation, and that my personal taste will at once recognize it and claim it when it comes forth. So I will let it alone, let it cook a little longer, wait for it. But the book itself would be fundamentally the same, and the man writing it the same as the child who wrote it. A certain maturity of taste, judgement and experience has taken place in the meantime, and that is all.

Here I am, then, a person believed to be adult, certainly more than old enough to be, and certainly experienced enough in my tastes and responsibilities, yet engaged professionally in the business of writing and drawing pictures for children. Why on earth do I do it? Why do I not address myself to adults like myself? Am I, perhaps, a teacher – for that, after all, would naturally explain a certain professional habit of mind towards The Young. But no, I am not and never have been a teacher, and indeed the experience of my childhood has, I regret to say, inclined me to regard teachers, *ab initio*, with a most unreasonable degree of fear and mistrust. (To any teacher who may be reading this I apologize sincerely. I am learning to overcome the prejudice.) No, I would regard the educative element in my work as only marginal, as is the case, I believe, with most if not all 'children's writers'. So I repeat and expand the question: What are we all doing, we children's writers, spending the precious life-drops of our professional time and energy in writing books for young readers? Have we our tongues in our cheeks? Are we hoping for an easy success by catering below our best standards to ignorant, inexperienced or immature persons? Certainly not. What, then, *is* the motivation?

Now I am aware that I have undertaken here to write briefly about myself and my work, and it may be asked why I seem to be discussing something else: not *how* I do my work, but *why*. Surely, though, that is the more important part of the question. As to how I do it, the answer is, quite truthfully, that I do not know. My work, given that I apply the daily discipline of sitting down to do it, brings itself up and out of me with all its good, bad and indifferent parts together, with all its own difficulties and facilities, winding out of the matrix of my own character in a manner which I can recognize, too often with regret, but which I cannot explain, and over which I have all too little control. So I cannot say how; but I repeat, the only really interesting part of the question is not how, but why I do it. And since, as I suggested at the beginning of this essay, all people are alike in being somewhat odd, and since all writers are alike in being similarly oddified in their work, it may be that many children's writers will agree that their own reasons for doing what they do are not very dissimilar from mine.

Let me put my case, then, in a nutshell. I do not write *for* children at all. As I have already told you, I do not really believe that children exist, except in the rather special sense of their comparative inexperience. I make allowances for this inexperience in my writing. It would probably be a waste of time, for example, to write much or anything in a children's book about questions of sexual conduct or morality, since children's experience in these matters is too limited for useful or interesting artistic development. But since the range of adult books seems at the present time to be concerning itself more and more with these matters, almost one might suppose to the exclusion of anything else, this does tend to mean that if you want to write about anything else in a fictional sort of way, children are soon going to be about the only people left to write for. But this doesn't mean that one has to write for them *as* children. One does not speak to the childish part of them, but to the adult part. There is an aphorism of Cyril Connolly's, that inside every fat man there is a thin man trying to get out. In the same way, inside every child there is an adult trying to get out, trying to find a common ground with adults upon which he (or she) can expand and grow. What is this common ground?

I will answer for myself. I look back to the little boy who wrote *Walks in our Museums* and I perceive in him a daydreaming reaching-out towards all historical things, all historical objects, all historical subjects, and all reconstructions and representations of these in books, theatres and cinemas. I see very little difference between the daydreams and the aptitudes of that little boy and of the man who a few years ago wrote and illustrated a children's book reconstructing the life of *Shakespeare's Theatre*. The only difference is that I had a certain amount of success with *Shakespeare's Theatre*, whereas *Walks in Our Museums* was received by my elders with what I can only recall as a sort of surprised amusement (very damnable and patronizing, now I come to think of it). The manuscript was eventually lost. Probably some housemaid (there were still a few housemaids around in those days, at preparatory schools) lit the fire with it, as happened with Carlyle's *French Revolution*. If so, I imagine it didn't do very well, even as a firelighter. It wasn't a very big exercise book, and I don't think cream-laid paper lights very good fires.

But let me not wander from the point. I am seeking a common ground between adult and child, for the writing of children's books. In my own case I have found one in a common subject matter, a love of history. But what of style? I look back to the books that I read and was hypnotized by as a child, and bit my nails over, half way up to my elbows: *Harold* by Bulwer Lytton, Whyte Melville's *The Gladiators*, Kingsley's *Hereward the Wake* . . . And then, with an awful horror of recognition, I turn to a book about King Alfred I once wrote and published, and I find therein all these same romantic Victorian ingredients – the dark skies, the ominous cawing of ravens, the shields lying split on the battlefield, the webs of fate and the dawns of hope and the trumpets in the mist and all that. I am writing stories for that same little boy I used to be, who used to read *Hereward the Wake*. It seems he was not fully satisfied, and I am trying to make it up to him. I am writing in every sense for myself. I suggest we are all writing for ourselves. For if in every child there is an adult trying to get out, equally in every adult there is a child trying to get back. On the overlapping of those two, *there* is the common ground.

# 6

## SEEING GREEN
### *Jill Paton Walsh*

MOST of the writers who have contributed to the spectacular flowering of children's literature in our time have been heard to say at some moment or another that they do not write for children. They write for themselves, or for the child they once were, or for anyone. 'For children about your age,' I say myself, when some adult asks me what age I write for. This attitude, which irritates some people beyond endurance, is not found only among the writers of books for the nearly grown-up, the publishers' eleven-plus category; it extends to many who write for the very small, and to illustrators of picture books, too. One of the most illuminating judgements of children's writers, in fact, is to sort out which of them really are writing 'for children' in any non-mystical sense.

Some writers, of course, do just that. They are interested in children. They think of their audience, and tailor what they have to say to fit their concept of that audience's needs and capacities. There is no need to be condescending about that. Children do have needs, and one of the basic duties of adult humanity is to provide for them. The book about going into hospital, or starting school, or getting along with your brothers and sisters is a perfectly worthy equivalent of the holding of hands, wiping of sticky fingers, or the cooking of fish-fingers that the loving care of children demands. In theory, there is no reason why a book written for children in this sense should not be truly disinterested; but in practice there is no escaping the fact that most which are, like most of the activities of parents and teachers, are manipulative. They are written in much the same spirit as that in which we offer green vegetables. 'It's good for you,' or, if the recipient is protesting strongly, 'It's for *your own good*.'

It is probably annoyance at being constantly taken for parents and pedagogues, thought of as providers of literary fish-fingers, that makes so many of us forceful in denying that we give a damn about children – which denial is almost the only form of pretentiousness common amongst us.

For many contemporary writers, myself included, write for children not because we are interested in children – though of course, on the side, some of us are – and not at all because we wish to shape, influence or educate anybody; but because our aesthetic preferences, our character and temperament have led us to like the sort of literature that children also like, or are thought to like, even if it is a kind of literature that is disdainfully thought of as childish by the modish and intellectual among our contemporaries. It is my strongly held opinion that the kind of book I try to write, and which many of my contemporaries write brilliantly – the fine 'children's book' – can be written well only by people who like that kind of thing for itself, and for themselves, and do not see it as any kind of come-down or any kind of educational tool. If they have had a good grounding in English Literature, for instance, the chances are they will like border ballads and carols better than court poetry, medieval narrative poems better than Spenser, Shakespeare better than Jonson – well, that one is fairly usual, after all! – the *Odyssey* better than the *Aeneid*. The thing has, in short, a discernible aesthetic, is one possible sort of taste in literature.

It is, as far as I can see, not an unusual taste at all. The audience for children's books consists of children, together with a motley assortment of adults who, because of their interest in children, parental or professional, have happened to come across children's books. Some of these adult readers, avid and enthusiastic as they appear to be, do not read much contemporary adult fiction. Even more of them read only books from other lowly categories: science fiction, detective stories, romances and historical novels. The serious novel seems to say nothing to them at all. They are not unliterary. We have all, I expect, met them; – they come forward eagerly to talk to us, bringing their children as excuse and disguise. They are the missing mass audience that sustained the novel of the last century, and has been lost in ours.

A contempt for this mass audience, a belief that what appeals to them cannot be good, is one of the less amiable marks of the high culture of our century. Children's writers know all about that – there is a similar belief around that something written for children is necessarily inferior, could not be a serious work of art. People who in the midst of a profound philosophical debate will let 'But glory doesn't mean a nice knock-down argument!' run trippingly off their tongues, will still often think that children's books are the nursery slopes of the mind's mountains, on which a writer will linger only if he lacks the courage and skill to do something better. 'When are you going to write a real book?' is asked of us too often to be a joke.

I suppose that it is because literature is so abstract that people evince so little common sense about it. For children's writers, like other writers, practise a craft. I don't imagine many people think that a children's doctor need not be so good at medicine as his colleagues, or that a carpenter who makes toys can manage with shoddy joinery. The truth is that a book which is bad literature just doesn't have much effect of any kind: doesn't work for anyone, old or young. Like any other writer, a children's writer has got to be good.

It isn't even true that there is somehow a different sort of goodness appropriate to children's books. The problems and the satisfactions of the writer-craftsman working for children are mainstream problems, mainstream satisfactions. I am taking it for granted that an adult writer will seek to embody and communicate adult insights in his books, will not solve problems by talking down to his audience. That being so, one might think that the writer for children has a much greater problem in getting himself understood. But that thought underestimates children, and over-values understanding. One doesn't specially want a child reader to understand intellectually, to (as it were) decode the message in a work of fiction. After all, he doesn't – God keep us from it! – have to sit an examination on his reading. It is enough, it is better, if the reader simply experiences the book, simply feels it. And a reader can feel truly on very partial understanding. I will instance my own children watching the televised *War and Peace*. When Natasha met clandestinely with Kuriagin they became deeply agitated. She couldn't! – what would happen? – what about Prince Andre? – oh dear no! Of course, they couldn't understand the passion that motivated Natasha; they saw it as entirely a question of loyalty. But it *is* that, among other things. They see only part of the whole, but what they do see is seen truly, is not distorted. Fully understanding a book is too often like being led forward in front of a pointilliste painting, and shown how the green is made up of spots of pure blue and pure yellow. One 'understands', but one can no longer seen green.

I can do without being understood as long as the reader sees green. The problem of being comprehensible is an emotional, an aesthetic problem – that of making the book adequately embody its meaning: that of getting the reader to 'see green' and making the seeing of green, just thus and then, emotionally meaningful. This is a central problem in literary art, not at all unlike the problem of Dickens, confronting his mass readership, or of anyone else confronting even the most elite audience.

Of course, the audience of children, or the adult masses, have their tastes – they have an insatiable appetite for narrative. That appetite is not looked on with favour in the high culture. From the mass of books of literary criticism one quickly learns to think that narrative is a sort of crude clothes peg for hanging up the stuff that really matters, and is really deep – symbol, image, characterization, social observation, theme. If that were true it would also be true that children's books, which are far more exclusively narrative than mainstream novels, were doomed to swim in shallow waters. But it cannot for long escape the working writer, however much Lit. Crit. he is stuffed with before he starts, that a narrative is itself an image. It is a linear image, extended in time. It is an image of a sequence of changes. It can be coherent or incoherent, significant or silly, ugly or beautiful in itself. When superlatively executed it carries a full charge of meaning, becomes incandescent in the mind.

Rather elaborate though it is, I shall resort to the image of the cave in Plato's *Republic*. The child reader is like the captive in the cave, chained so that he can look only towards the wall, and knowing nothing of the reality outside. But he can see the shadows cast by passing objects on the wall of the cave. Those shadows have depth and texture. But a narrative simply draws a line round them, makes an outline. Even an outline has the one essential quality of art – it has significant form. The simplest children's book has that, if it is any good.

The task of making simple significant narrations is a task with a long history. Homer turned his hand to it, and innumerable poets and novelists since. If it is no longer what many novelists want their work to achieve, it is still not a thing for anyone to condescend to. The best writer might measure his talents against it with humility. And when, rarely, someone succeeds, and a true masterpiece is produced, it will always be something that the child who reads it takes on with him into adult life. It's like that old saying that strategy is too important to leave to generals; any book that is good enough for children is too good to leave only to them.

As I said earlier, children's writers practise a craft. We try to be good enough.

# 7

# THE IMPRISONED CHILD

## *Nina Bawden*

W HEN I started to write it never occurred to me to write for children. I wrote *about* them, for adults, partly because the child's viewpoint is (as Henry James knew) a sly way of commenting on adult society, and partly because I remembered my own childhood so vividly, particularly the frustrations of being a child. Children think and feel deeply, in some ways more deeply than adults, but they cannot express their thoughts and feelings effectively. Because they are ignorant, their opinions are thought to be valueless; because they cannot act to any purpose, they are forced to be lookers-on, dependent on the uncertain whims of the adults about them.

The first child I ever wrote about was a fat, plain, nine-year-old liar who was involved with a murderer. Because he has a club foot she thinks of him as the Devil, and because she knows herself to be wicked, she is both attracted and repelled by him. She tries to tell her parents what is happening to her; but her story is such a muddle of fact and fantasy that they cannot understand and assume she is lying as usual. I used this child to give a turn of the screw to a thriller, but she was part of me, of my remembered past; and as I wrote about her, and about other children in later novels for adults, I began to feel indignant on behalf of the child I had been, and so on behalf of all children – those passionately aware human beings imprisoned in a uniquely humiliating disguise.

To write for children was a logical development for me. I wanted to write, not as a grown-up looking back, but as a former child, remembering the emotional landscape I had once moved in, how I had felt, what concerned me, what I wanted to know. The books I would write would be adventures, of course. All children love adventures: and not just for the what-happens-next excitement. You don't have to read Freud to know that children enjoy Jack killing the giant. But more important still is the mental exercise an adventure story can give them. Even if you write realistically and don't allow your young hero or heroine to win out against a gang of desperate men, you can still present them with a situation in which they can see themselves, against which they can test their own courage. Would they be brave if this happened to them, or would they run away? Would they be honest, or would they lie?

Children are interested in moral questions. Their judgements may be over-simplified – good or bad, black or white – and based on limited knowledge, but this doesn't necessarily detract from their value: to know too much sometimes confuses the issue. The adult will often flounder about in the shallow while the child dives in at the deep end . . .

Not that the child's point of view is unsubtle. Children are detached, attentive observers. Although they may not comprehend, altogether, the events that are taking place in front of their eyes, what they do see they see clearly – goodness and virtue as well as cant and hypocrisy – and they are fascinated by the endless variety in human behaviour. People are not statistics, faces in a crowd, but individuals, awkward, quirky, never one like another.

This interest in character – an unfashionable one in adult fiction just now – is one of the reasons I enjoy writing for children. I find it rewarding to look at the adults around me from their point of view, see what they see – which is often a less agreeable picture than the one adults have of themselves – and set it down for them, tell my tale through their eyes, from their *side*.

A straightforward enough recipe, it seemed, when I started. A pleasure for me, and apparently for children too: they wrote and said so. But there is more to writing for children than this simple relationship between writer and reader, because children don't buy the books they are given to read. If you write children's novels there is an enormous army of librarians, teachers, reviewers and booksellers between you and your audience; and although I knew this in principle, I didn't realize the effect this could have on a writer until I began to be asked to talk about my work to educational conferences. I have enjoyed doing this – there is usually pleasure in explaining one's craft – but recently I have begun to feel a growing bewilderment bordering on a kind of despair. Speaking to people who care, often deeply, for children, I have begun to feel that the *child* I write for is mysteriously absent . . .

'Are you concerned, when you write, to see that the girls are not forced into feminine role-playing?' 'What about the sexuality of children?' 'All writers are middle class, at least by the time they have become successful as writers, so what use are their books to working-class/deprived/emotionally or educationally backward children?' 'Writers should write about modern [*sic*] problems, like drugs, schoolgirl pregnancies. Aren't the books you write rather escapist?' 'What do you know about the problems of the child in the high-rise flat since you have not lived in one?'

To take this last question. The reply, that you project your imagination, is seldom taken as adequate; but what other one is there? I have seen my own bewilderment reflected in the faces of other writers on the same platform, and heard it in the answers they gave. How can you explain, intellectually, what is done by instinct? All any writer can do is write the books that are in him; his only duty is to write them as well as he can. And above all, how can you explain that the child you are writing for doesn't live in a slum or a mansion, that he is neither deprived nor privileged, but a being so strange and incalculably varied in his responses, so infinitely capable of development in astonishing ways, that all you can properly do is tell him the story you have in your mind and leave him to take what he wants from it?

Listening to all these unanswerable – because, to me, basically irrelevant – questions, I find myself growing indignant again on the children's behalf. It seems to me that what a great many of these good, well-meaning adults are doing is precisely what I objected to in the first place: undervaluing the child, seeing him as an object in a sociological survey, an unformed creature without will or thought of his own, to be tamed, educated, never learned *from* – forced into their way of thinking.

Well, that isn't my job. I am not a teacher nor a branch of the social services, and I find it confusing to see myself regarded that way. So confusing that I have begun to feel that if I go on talking or writing about writing for children I shall lose sight of – and therefore betray, in a sense – the child I am writing for.

# 8

# THOUGHTS ON
# BEING AND WRITING

*Russell Hoban*

LIFE presents itself to us daily, and not content with that, goes on to do it nightly as well. Of this continuous presentation we make what sense we can – mostly very little. It's difficult to know who's looking out through the eyeholes in our faces and it's difficult to know what's being looked at. For security we put our little single sensings together in one big consensus. But no sooner is the security of that consensus gained than loss is felt. It is the loss of the clean risk and constant danger of perception. Make us perceive again, we say, and open the door to the artist, who thanks us and blows the house up the best he can.

To repeat, life is a continuous presentation of sensation and event. Faced with that presentation and faced with himself facing it, the artist re-presents it. Why? He can't help it; his representation is part of the presentation. It is an action of the awareness through which life manifests itself. Even the form of matter is itself a kind of awareness: a stone, unconscious as it may be, is the awareness of the atoms maintaining the formal substance of the stone. A human being, even before consciousness or thought, is the awareness imprinted on the cells that maintain the formal substance of the human being. A society is the awareness of the people who maintain its formal substance according to the image of society imprinted on them. That collective awareness is made up of many individual awarenesses which do not appear to be functionally different as, for example, the cells of the body are. Yet in action the awarenesses differ: some hold the shape of things; some alter; some build; some destroy. All change constantly, and the formal substance of societies and civilizations changes with those changing awarenesses.

Man seems to be driven, in his one-way passage through time, through cycles of order and chaos that pursue each other like subject and answer in a musical fugue. And now we seem to be in the stretto of our time – the tight place, the place that is narrow, close, pressed together like the overlapping of fugal subject and answer. This century is almost four-fifths gone. Its years and its days are dwindling to a point, as are the resources of this planet.

We long for order, but it may be that order is no longer definable. In a report of a quantum theory colloquium at Cambridge I read that 'Ordering is a primitive term which has no fixed content . . . there is no such thing as disorder: whatever happens is ordering.' And Marlowe's Mephistophilis says to Doctor Faustus:

> Hell hath no limits, nor is circumscribed
> In one self place; for where we are is hell,
> And where hell is there must we ever be:
> And, to conclude, when all the world dissolves,
> And every creature shall be purified,
> All places shall be hell that is not heaven.

Both statements seem to be descriptive of our situation.

George Steiner, in his essay, *In Bluebeard's Castle*, speaks of 'the image we carry of a lost coherence, of a centre that held.' He also says:

Because it carries the past within it, language, unlike mathematics, draws backward. This is the meaning of Eurydice. Because the realness of his inward being lies at his back, the man of words, the singer, will turn back, to the place of necessary, beloved shadows. For the scientist, time and light lie before.

It seems to me that that 'lost coherence', the image of which we do indeed carry, is not the order of an earlier and better time but the original order of inanimate matter. And our constant longing for it is what Freud has described as the death instinct, 'the urge inherent in organic life to restore an earlier state of things which the living entity has been obliged to abandon under the pressure of external disturbing force'. The inanimate was disturbed into the animate, non-life was disturbed into life, and in us is a longing for the peace that was before that original disturbance. In all of us, I think, there remains some awareness, rudimentary and inchoate, far down, dim in green light through the ancient reeds and tasting of the primal salt, in which there is no 'I', no person, no identity, but only the passage, moment by moment, of time through being undisturbed by birth or death. We push away from it but it is there, containing self and struggle both. Far down and dim it is, not ordinarily accessible to us. I think we have to learn to feel for it, to go beyond our swimmer's fright, to dive for it and touch it before returning to the sunlight and the present, to touch it as a child in a dark room gets out of bed to touch the clothes tree that bulks monstrous in the dimness, magnetic with terror.

Language does, of course, carry the past in it, but the man of words need not always turn back, or need not *only* turn back. Orpheus he must be, perhaps, but he can be Daedalus as well; he *must* be Daedalus because it is his nature thus to be. Always, as Orpheus, he must look back and lose Eurydice; always as Daedalus he must see Icarus fall into the sea. Always he must live his days bereaved.

No poet, no artist of any art, has his complete meaning alone . . . what happens when a new work of art is created is something that happens simultaneously to all the works of art which preceded it . . . the whole existing order must be, if ever so slightly, altered; and so the relations, proportions, values of each work of art towards the whole must be readjusted . . . Whoever has approved this idea of order, of the form of European, of English literature, will not find it preposterous that the past should be altered by the present as much as the present is directed by the past. And the poet who is aware of this will be aware of the great difficulties and responsibilities.

What is to be insisted upon is that the poet must develop or procure the consciousness of the past and that he should continue to develop this conscious-ness throughout his career. What happens is a continual surrender of himself as he is at the moment to something which is more valuable. The progress of an artist is a continual self-sacrifice, a continual extinction of personality.

It is in this depersonalization that art may be said to approach the condition of science.

Thus T. S. Eliot in a 1919 essay answers Steiner's 1971 comment (made in a T. S. Eliot Memorial Lecture) about the man of words who turns back to the shadows and the scientist for whom time and the light lie before.

Now I want to consider what Eliot says about new and old works of art: 'What happens when a new work of art is created,' he says, 'is some-thing that happens simultaneously to all the works of art which preceded it.' I find myself wanting to see that demonstrated physically.

I imagine a large, empty room into which, one by one, are brought works of art from different times and different places. The first piece I think of is the *Willendorf Venus*, a little prehistoric female figure carved in tawny-reddish limestone. I have never seen it, only its picture in a book. It's only about four inches high, almost faceless, all belly and breasts. The profound exaggeration of its simplicity intensifies its little ancient silence.

In the world of the imagined room it is the only art there is, the only representation of human reality. The woman of flesh of that time is not; the stone woman-symbol is. It refers to what I know and what I don't know. It is, and it refers to what is not. It commands the time, the space of the room, and me. It is the product of a way of seeing; in it are the seer and the seen, both gone. The seeing and the being seen remain, made solid in the stone. There are voices in it. Are there words? Breath there was, and hands that touched. Does this Venus look forward to words? Was there possibly a time when words were unshaped, unborn, carried in the future? Here is a symbol of flesh, of carnal knowledge, of birth and ongoing life. Here is a symbol referring to men and women and children, to voices, mornings, nights, and rain. Fire, certainly. But perhaps no words. That must be impossible; if seeing became this art, then speech must have become words. The words heard by her are in her, everything up to the time that is her present time is in her; it is impossible to contain all that she contains.

Now an arm from some lost colossal Egyptian statue is brought into the room. A stone arm fifteen feet long with an implacable stone fist at the end of it. This stone was quarried somewhere, lifted, moved. Scribes wrote down its transport and consignment.

What now? What are you now, little Venus of Willendorf? Tiny in the big room, lit from all sides you lie with overlapping shadows radiating from you. Lit by the same lights and casting shadows of the same density, this colossal arm lies with you. Dark in the rearward obscurity of time, someone holds you in his hand, finds your breasts and belly in the stone warm with the warmth of his hand. Bright in the implacable rearward brilliance of sunlit time, ropes and ramps move quarried stone. A scribe sits cross-legged and writes. The room is full of the colossal absent statue; the room is shattered by the silence of that present stone fist.

Now who are you, Venus of Willendorf, and who am I? The arm knows who it is. The arm is not it, but *they*. The arm is multitudes. Venus is *they* also, more so than before. The multitudes of Egyptians have called up all the little horde of Venus, all the hunters, their women and their children. They rise up in an ancient mist of morning, among the barking of dogs and the smoke of cooking fires. They are compelled by the colossal arm to present themselves.

The colossal arm speaks of its polishing, its chisel strokes and its mallet blows. Chisel and mallet evoke an arm of flesh and bone, an arm not colossal, many arms not colossal, many figures not colossal, facing speech-less the hunters and their women and their children. *You,* say the silent faces of the hunters. *This,* says the force that moved the arms that held the chisel and the mallet. *This,* says the life in Venus's stone belly.

Am I in the room at all now? Have I the power to be equally present? The colossal arm and the little Venus have each compelled the other to call up its people and its time, its innumerable self. Now I too am thrust forward by generations jostling behind me, offering Bibles and printing presses, aeroplanes, bombs and telephones. Venus must again move forward to meet me, to maintain the connection. So must the colossal arm. Both must intensify and multiply, to displace volumes of time equal to those behind me so they can be present with me. What if I had not had the power to be equally present? What if Venus had not been able to displace the necessary volumes of time to maintain her presence with me?

I was going to bring other objects into the room, from other times and places. But these two are enough. I can't explain what has happened. I've showed it to the reader, and that must suffice.

I'm beginning to have an idea of what I'm writing about and why I'm writing at all. 'Equally present,' I said. Have I the power to be equally present? Life, living itself through Venus's people, through the non-colossal Egyptians, flows on through me with its illimitable power. I have no choice but to be a channel for it, to be used for birth and death and procreation and mallet blows, and I must exert more strength and cunning than did Venus's people or the Egyptians, because I encounter a greater accumulation of time and lives than they. So I must put forth a greater effort, because that is the task laid upon me by life – to be equally present.

Depersonalization, Eliot said. Time and the light lying before, said Steiner. Life is using me as a channel for birth and death and procreation and mallet blows, I said. Now I have to tell you about the birth of my fifth child, the child of a new relationship in this country that is new to me.

For the first time I was present all through the labour. In the delivery room I was given a mask and gown and so was able to keep an eye on the business end of things while I cheered Gundula on and told her when to bear down and when to let up. Simply from an engineering point of view, the whole project seemed unlikely. I've spoken of the stretto of our time, but the original stretto, the passageway to life, the primal tight place for each individual one of us, is really a remarkably tight place for a new person to get through. Gundula bore down and let up as required, after strong exertions a head appeared, cleverly guided by the doctor, the shoulder turned, and blip! there was a new boy in the world, bluish and clayey-looking, still roped to his mother by the thick umbilical cord. Twenty or so student nurses who'd been led into the room observed but did not applaud. The cord was cut, the boy was held up by the ankles and squalled like a cat whose tail has been stepped on. The midwife sucked out the mucus, put drops in his eyes, weighed him, wrote up a ticket. 'Eight pounds, eight ounces,' she said. 'Have you got a name for him?'

'Jachin,' I said. Jachin was the name of one of the pillars that stood in front of Solomon's temple. The other was named Boaz. This boy's name is Jachin Boaz Hoban.

At other births I have paced and smoked in waiting rooms until the time came when I could see, among ranks of infants in a display behind glass, the cleaned-up one that was mine. And I have thought sentimental thoughts about 'my child' and what the future would bring and so forth. This time was different. I had been where moments followed one by one in an unbroken flow from ocean and the primal salt, from far back, far down where the light was dim and green through ancient reeds. Life, continuous from there, big in the belly of the little Venus, mighty in the stone colossal arm, is a savage and practical thing that invents placentas and umbilical cords to keep itself going. And life has used Gundula and me to bring Jachin into the morning mist and the noonday sun with Venus's people and the non-colossal Egyptians. He's life's child before and after everything else; he does not personally belong to Gundula and me. He's ours to love and have fun with and take care of until he can take care of himself, but he's not really ours, and both of us know it.

'The poet must surrender himself as he is at the moment to something which is more valuable,' says Eliot. 'The progress of the artist is a continual self-sacrifice, a continual extinction of personality.' Well, it takes a real high-flying intellectual to come up with something that elementary. What else, really, could the progress of an artist possibly be? Art, like babies, is one of the things life makes us make, and the strongest, most passionate affirmation of the self is necessarily the losing of the self in that continuous stream of being in which we change the past and the past changes us. The babies don't belong to us and neither does the art, because what can the most powerful integration of self with life be but the dropping of that precious fussy little identity that we wear like morning dress and a bowler hat? For goodness' sake forget it. And once it's for-gotten, time and the light are now. And the next moment and the moment after that.

Well, here we are in the stretto, as I've said. Life continues its changing balance of war and peace, famine and plenty, hope and despair, and the devaluation of currencies and people. Are writers moving forward to-wards time and the light? Are they achieving that affirmative extinction of personality, that necessary symbiosis with the past? Some are, I think, particularly those who write for children and young people.

I don't read many contemporary novels, but sometimes I talk to people who do. It seems to me and some of my friends that more and more adult novels are not essentially literary. Many of them simply communicate experience, and that of itself is not art. To attempt to define the literary art is not my purpose here, but I think it always has in it the action de-scribed in my exercise with the *Willendorf Venus* and the colossal Egyp-tian arm: it makes us be equally present in a continuous flow of time and being and it evokes vital resources in us. There are empty spaces now in literature, vacated by the so-called adult novel, and some of those spaces now become new territory for children's writers. I cannot offer a broad objective survey, but I have some highly subjective comments to make on three writers.

John Christopher has written many adult novels, but none so good, in my opinion, as his books for young people. I think the best of his recent books is *The Guardians*, which is essentially a political book. Christopher is well aware that there is no such thing as a non-political act; whatever we do is political in that it is either for or against the established system of our culture.

Dissent and revolution are natural expressions of the human competitor, and always represent chances for new patterns. I'll even go so far as to say that the unpredictable action of the dissenting competitor is the best hope of the human race. Going by mathematical probabilities, nothing predictable is going to help us, so we can only hope for something that can't be predicted. From whom? Well, there's nobody here but us, is there? Young us, middle-aged us, and old us.

It's young us that Christopher writes about in *The Guardians*, the soli-tary outsider, the lone maverick. In the year 2052 thirteen-year-old Rob Randall lives in the anti-intellectual London Conurb with its crowds and riots and sports spectacles. His mother is dead, and after the apparently accidental death of his father he is sent to a state boarding-school. After being censured for the possession of books he is sadistically punished by his schoolfellows, and runs away to the County, the world of the gentry where his mother had once been a servant. Christopher puts his story together with archetypal elements – the pressure of the group on the individual; the flight of the outsider to the Green Belt, the mother-place, the earth place where he will undergo the trial of finding the self he must be. To reach the Green Belt he must cross the no-man's-land that divides it from the Conurb:

People, he knew, did not like living over by no-man's-land. That was why the houses had not been pulled down but left to rot: if they were demolished there would be a new edge and people would move away from that in turn. Rob found himself shivering, not just with the cold but at the sight of darkness, at the thought of the emptiness beyond. All his life, like everyone else in the Con-urbs, he had been surrounded by the comforting presence of others – all the millions of them.

The fear of the edge and the necessity of going over it is what is being looked into in this book. All of us like to move away from the edge be-cause the edge makes us uncomfortable. And at the same time the old atavistic hunting spirit in us drives us towards the edge. It's a double bind, really: if we don't go to the edge and over it as explorers, we go over it as hapless victims, because when we stand passive and still, time moves to-wards us and brings the edge with it. Man's lot is not, I think, to be com-fortable except in the active encounter with discomfort.

What precisely the edge is may vary for each of us, but each of us in-fallibly recognizes it. It's worth remembering that the world in men's minds was flat before the present round model was developed. People were afraid of going over the edge. Most of us now perceive the external world as being round and continuous – the edges are within us.

In this story Rob Randall finds in the Green Belt a costly illusion of safe well-being in which the roles and accoutrements of stylish gentility are maintained anachronistically: there are hunts and garden parties; well-sprung carriages roll smoothly on plastic roads. But brain surgery keeps the county gentlemen peaceful and good-humoured, and a power elite runs the whole thing. Given the chance to remain mentally virile as a member of the Guardian group, Rob decides to go his own more human and more dangerous way. He finds his integrity in that extinction of the personality, that surrender of self to something more valuable, that Eliot insists on. John Christopher, with complete psychological verity and no indulgence in heroics, has written a book of considerable depth and utility.

William Mayne, in *A Game of Dark*, has taken on not only the Oedipal conflict but the basic existential one of staying or going, holding on or splitting. Fourteen-year-old Donald Jackson lives with his crippled father and a mother who teaches at the school he attends and calls him by his surname as frequently as his Christian one. His dead sister is a constant shadowy presence. The atmosphere is piously oppressive and psychically corrupt.

Appropriately the story opens with a feeling of sickness and a pervasive stench. The bad smell of Donald's life has carried over into a second life in which he must ultimately fight a stinking worm who leaves a slimy track behind him as he preys on a feudal village. Needing to be a man, Donald drifts into a world where he is needed as a man. He rescues a girl who is reminiscent of his dead sister, and he is pressed into the service of the local lord. He can live in either of his two lives:

For a moment he could choose again which he would be. One is real, he said to himself. Donald is real. The other is a game of darkness, and I can be either and step from one to the other as I like. So he chose to stay on the sleeping shelf [in the feudal village], without knowing how completely he became the person there. When he had come back to the dark he was thoroughly the boy from the north who was walking southwards to see what he found. He was no longer Donald, but only the son of Jack, the same character but a different person. He had the choice of which to be, but it was one or the other. Neither person had the resources of the other, no more than the smallest memory, or perhaps vestigial awareness, of the other's existence.

He settled to sleep. Jackson. The dog sighed in his ear. The house slept.

From the outside there came again the wailing cry, rising and falling in the dark, bubbling in itself and in its echo.

Mayne is technically unlimited – he can do anything with words – and he handles his psychical shifts suavely. For a time Donald chooses the second life in the feudal village. Eventually he kills the worm, not in the proper knightly fashion but with the ingenuity and tenacity of desperate courage. At the end of the book people assume workable places:

Carrica was not his. She was his mother or his sister, and of those two he knew which was which, and he knew that the man in the other room was his father, whom he knew now how to love. Carrica was a phantom if he wanted her to be, and the house in Hales Hill was another, and he had the choice of which to remain with.

Donald finally chooses the world of everyday reality, and his father conveniently dies.

Mayne has taken on themes that require considerable force and depth of the writer; how well he has done with them is less important to me than that he regards them as being within his province.

Leon Garfield is an example of what talent can do to a children's book writer: it can drive him out of children's books as he follows the development of his material wherever it takes him, and that is precisely what's happened. *The Strange Affair of Adelaide Harris,* for instance, has to be considered as an adult book. Comedy is a serious business in that it relies on dead accuracy of insight – the laughs don't happen unless we recognize ourselves and others in each situation. And the depth of recognition for *Adelaide Harris* requires adult experience.

Garfield's outstanding characteristic has always been energy and exuberance, his gusto in using words; and this has sometimes led him into overwriting. In *The Ghost Downstairs*, however, after a characteristically twinkling opening, he settles into what I think is his best and tightest writing to date. His variation of the Faust legend is a conception of frightening power, and wholly a book for grownups.

The measure of his invention is the shocking vitality of his 'What if?': What if it isn't necessarily the Devil who wants to buy the soul of Mr Fast? What if the canny seller offers the mysterious Mr Fishbane seven years of his life in return for wealth, but seven years from the *beginning* of it? What if, having signed away with his childhood all that was bright and wondrous in him, he finds existence a perdition of betrayal through which he haplessly pursues the self that he has sold?

In this book the theme has dominated the writer and freed him from mannerism and self-consciousness. His sensitivities are heightened, his sense of detail is remarkable: the sound of an iron hoop rolled by the ghost of childhood; a marvellous model of St Paul's made by a cabinetmaker 'long since retired from life size', with the craftsman's giant spectacles lying on miniature Ludgate Hill; the 'gently outstretched hands' of a young man sleeping in a train compartment – darks and lights evolved within the reader build a shifting chiaroscuro through which moments flash occulting one by one until the end:

'Where shall we go now?' whispered the little phantom, its pale face smiling up into the old man's.

'God knows', answered Mr Fishbane, and his beard streamed out to catch the stars.

The echo of Marlowe's 'See, see where Christ's blood streams in the firmament!' is not out of place; it closes a book that is eerily insightful, demonically vital, and not quite definable, a story in which the unhappy present destroys itself by betraying the innocent past.

There are aspects of life that require not simply to be communicated as experience, but to be made into art, and if some writers won't do it then others will. I have cited only three, and of course it is not difficult to think of many more. The essential themes will always find both writers and readers. John Christopher has turned from adult novels to books for younger readers, finding the formal limitation a concentrating and strengthening element for his examination of life and manhood. William Mayne, long a first-rank children's writer, has recognized the writer's responsibility to engage whatever dragons come his way, however big. Leon Garfield has been driven by his talent out of the children's category into new writing of rare distinction.

All three of these books change the past. Because of John Christopher's Rob Randall, Huck Finn must take a new look around him and see that perhaps he is right and the world wrong. Because of William Mayne's Donald Jackson, the prehistoric boy in the dream life of the narrator of Jack London's book, *Before Adam*, moves forward, extends the distance from his dim beginnings. Because of Leon Garfield's Mr Fast, Marlowe's Faustus meets in himself a devil more terrifying than Mephistophilis.

As we move forward in this stretto of time the distinctions between children and adults blur and fade: today's children do not live in an ex-purgated world. With their elders they must endure sudden deaths and slow ones, bombs and fire falling from the sky, the poisoning of peaceful air and the threatened extinction of this green jewel of Earth. They must endure the reality of mortal man. Like Mr Fast in Leon Garfield's book we have sold the self that must at all costs be preserved and not betrayed. New selves arise each moment, and we must offer them a friendly hand of innocence and encouragement.

If in my meandering I have seemed to offer tangled thinking more than worked-out thoughts, it has not been through self-indulgence; I have wanted to join the action of my being with that of my readers in a collective being. Collectively we must possess and be repossessed by the past that we alter with our present, must surrender the vanity of personal identity to something more valuable. We must with our children go into the dark and through it to a place where time and the light lie before us.

# MRS HOOKANEYE AND I

## *Jane Gardam*

ONE of the great surprises when you begin to write fiction in middle age is the questions you get asked. You can cope with the wide-eyed stares and frank disbelief. In fact, they are rather pleasant. What you cannot cope with is the questioning – utterly astounding, unanswerable questioning from people you have known or thought you have known these twenty years.

'How do you think of your plots?', for instance. (Well, answer me that!)

'How do you think up the people? Is it yourself?' is another. The most usual.

Yet another – and I have taken to answering 'yes' to this one though I'm really not sure about it at all – is, 'Oh, are they for *children*?'

'Yes.'

'Oh, I *see*.'

Mrs Hookaneye is comforted by this very much. Any old nut can write for children. She has thought of writing for children herself. What do I think of . . . ? And a long list of other writers for children follows, for Mrs Hookaneye has several children or grandchildren of her own, and spends money on good books for them. And oh dear! I don't know how other writers of books for the young feel: I only know, heaven help me, that I read very few children's books and that, with about three blazing exceptions, a serious impediment in my speech occurs when I am asked to talk about them.

A pause, then back to question two. 'Oh, the first little girl *was* you, wasn't she? The one in your first book. She does so remind me of you,' say Mrs Hookaneye, Mrs Pollywog, my mother's friend. 'It is you, isn't it?'

Only in so far as every hero is oneself. Only in so far as no hero in fiction can really be oneself. Autobiography is dangerous stuff. I can never see how anyone has the audacity to write autobiography until he has been famous a while. Even then it's usually better not to. No, dear Mrs Hookaneye, Mrs Toodles – not myself. I was never so fearless and strong, never so lucid and loving. I tied my little brother to a chair when he was two and went off to the pictures. I spent my days in endless fret at the impression I was making on people, drained by misery because everybody hated me. Don't you remember, Mrs H? You've known me since the pram.

'I knew from the first page, dear, that Lucy was you. And what a lovely picture of the town.'

And here I beam and embrace her and adore her: for yes, please, it is meant to be an attempt at the town and the landscape where I was brought up, in the North Riding by the sea which I loved and I love and I will love for ever. That is true. I can stand any amount of discussion about that. The trouble is that nobody but the other people in the town really wants to join in. You can't be too careful with regional passions. Unless you're a genius, watch out and remember Mary Webb. Joe Blogg's childhood looked as good as yours and mine to Joe Bloggs, and the same sun came creeping in at morn at his little window.

'*Just* like the town,' continues Mrs Hookaneye, 'but I don't quite remember all those people, Jane. A little poetic licence there, perhaps?'

'Well, yes,' says I.

For of course they weren't there. They just wandered in, some of them. Some were there. My beloved aunts were there, and the sea-coal woman on the beach (I think), and my father and the maid. But some wandered in from somewhere outside. They are all rather mixed up in my mind now, the real ones and the rest.

Where do characters come from, anyway? What a question! It is such private territory, such an undergrowth. All one knows, without a mighty search, is that they are there – the characters – urgent to get out, and that there is no point in writing fiction otherwise: unless one is very short of money, and then one might do better to take other and more lucrative employment.

I wrote my books, dear Mrs H, because I so badly wanted to write them. I think I would probably have died if I hadn't written *A Few Fair Days*. But do you understand what I'm talking about, Mrs Hook? Mrs Bobtail? Mrs Splendiferous?

And do you understand – before you start thundering out tales yourselves – and I tell you, it plays havoc with the ironing – do you understand that I was most unusually lucky in my publisher, who accepted my first book even after I had committed the insanity of telephoning her unintroduced to inform her that my first MS was on its way? ('Some poor mad lady,' she tells me she said to her secretary. 'Dear me!') She accepted the book and said was I thinking of another? I said I might now have written my book. She said no, and was right.

For in the first book there was a sort of seed of a second. I wanted to examine somebody growing up in the landscape I had described which was then partly removed from her by a war, and I had touched on this in the last page or two of my first book.

I wrote a few new chapters of this new book. They were no good, so I did them again. Then what I was doing got hold of me, and I could think of nothing else. The girl in the new book possessed me. When I'd finished with her – and what a small step on I'd got! How little I knew of her and what she would become and when; or if there is any when, or becoming – or real understanding! – ; when I'd finished with her, I felt quite lost.

She was as different from me, that girl in *A Long Way from Verona*, as any child could be. I was a mouse, at that age, sometimes a mouse and sometimes a clown. The point about Jessica Vye is that her dizziness is meant to amount at moments almost to genius. No genius about me. I was considered pretty dim at school until I was sixteen and met a Lance-Corporal in the Army Education Corps who wrote poetry and decided I should go to Cambridge.

But again.

And again.

'I think that you are writing about *yourself*, Jane,' says Mrs Hookaneye.

So I set out quite deliberately to sort out another girl – one who could not possibly be thought to be me. She had raised her stately head in *A Long Way from Verona* – called by another name and just drifting in for a minute. She was beautiful, clever and good, and I had been a bit interested by her. I felt that being beautiful, clever and good should not be held against her. I wanted to get at her, somehow – find out how she'd be if her lovely happy background in a marvellous Georgian Rectory near Wilton Woods, where I used to go to tea when I was about nine (I met her there once, though her teeth stuck out a bit) – how she'd be if she lost it all.

So off I went, very slowly this time, with Athene Price. I got a bit too taken up with her ugly sister on the way, I think, who rather threatened to take charge of the book; but I liked old Athene, too, in the end, and it was painful when I destroyed her. For destroyed she is, of course, poor duck. Gone, gone like fifteen wild Decembers – or fifteen rainy Augusts, anyway. Gone, my dear American psychiatric critic who went for me so vigorously. 'Gardam,' he says, 'suggests that Athene is no more than a "high-spirited animal".' Oh dear me, no, sir. It is much worse even than that.

What have I learned in three books? Not much. Mostly about my limitations. A little about form, perhaps – a few experiments. I think that it may be in form and structure that the twentieth century so-called 'children's book' might in time be in advance of the rest. The novel at present, apart from the 'children's novel', seems to me to be often literally as well as figuratively in rather poor shape.

I have learned to wait for reviews and read them quietly without physical sickness, though still with unease. I haven't learned much yet about living with what I'm writing. I haven't learned yet how to cope with Mrs H. How not to be lonely for talk of books. The illustrator of my first book, Peggy Fortnum, said to me, 'Don't ever talk about your work to outsiders. Let it be like a secret sin.' But I can't decide whether this is right or not. I rise from my desk every day at three thirty-five to collect my youngest child from school, and stand looking rather battered at the school gate. It would be wonderful to start talking about what is really in one's head instead of which day is the concert and do you want a pair of size twelve football boots. To talk about work again as one did at college.

But, of course, one can't. One doesn't. One chatters on and goes home and, yes, well I'm sorry: I did forget to buy the blasted crumpets. One wonders whether it's worth stumbling on with two ramshackle lives at once. But really in one's heart one knows that it is stupendous luck and happiness to be able to work at all at what makes one most content.

# BOOKMAKER AND PUNTER
## *Leon Garfield*

I CAN think of only three reasons (apart from money) why a novelist should write about writing; and none of them is strictly honourable. Firstly he may feel that his published work has not quite done him justice and he may wish to explain certain obscurities . . . thereby tacitly admitting that he has failed in the prime requisite of a user of words: he has not been clear. Secondly, he may feel he has been too easily understood – that a certain paucity of thought has been displayed for all to see – and he may wish to remedy it by cloudy nonsense, suggesting that there was more in his work than ever met the critic's or reader's eye. This latter reason is, perhaps, the more common of the two, particularly among those of us who are published for the young. A certain shame creeps in that our deepest thoughts make common ground with conkers and model aeroplanes. We feel we are worthy of better than that; we feel we are worthy of not being read at all, perhaps? I know a writer who fairly hugs himself with glee when readers puzzle over his tales and admit they can make nothing of them. I sometimes wonder if he is prepared to offer book tokens for the first correct solution?

I don't blame him, though. It's much more galling to be understood than to be an object of bafflement. But enough of that. It's necessary to come to the third reason before the construction of the piece has been completely forgotten and the reader is unnerved by the mention of 'thirdly'.

Thirdly, then, the writer may wish (either from vanity, persuasion or simple-minded affability) to give some account of how he writes for the instruction and benefit of youthful rivals so that they may avoid his errors, escape his pitfalls and generally write so much better than he does that no one will ever buy his books again and he will die in a garret, breadless and friendless, to be revived (in coffin-covers) for the next generation to revere as a saintly idiot.

'Where do you get your ideas from?'

'Mind your own business!'

'Please! I've paid my money and I'm entitled to some sort of value for it.'

'Very well. Inspiration, then. I sit all alone on an inaccessible mountain top and the Muses breathe in my ears.'

'Liar.'

'Don't they teach you manners nowadays?'

'I'm trying to learn them.'

'All right – all right. If you want the dull truth – like everyone else, I started by pinching ideas from other books until I was able to recognize the sort of idea that was capable of being expanded into a whole book of my own. Today I find such ideas more directly . . . even in television or the cinema, to say nothing of the city streets. It doesn't really matter. One picks up bits of ideas, like an inky magpie, and threads them together until they make something that looks, at first sight, new. It isn't new, of course; nothing is.'

'Is that all there is to it?'

'No, it bloody well isn't! Find out for yourself what it's like to see an old man in a pub shuffling off in search of the gents with one bleary eye fixed apprehensively on the half pint of bitter he's been forced to abandon to the call of nature; observe greed, fear and his own helpless physical nature all contending within his frail frame and shaking it almost to pieces. Observe all this and wonder how you can make use of the emotions it rouses within you while, at the same time, preserving what you have actually seen.'

'I don't go into pubs. I'm too young.'

'Try a Wimpy bar, then.'

'You're losing your temper. What price manners now?'

'Oh go to . . . the library!'

'That wasn't what you were going to say; but it's interesting – the way you punctuated it. Why did you use three dots instead of a dash?'

'Because I thought it looked better. Are you going to grow up into a critic?'

'I don't know yet. I just mean to grow up.'

'The way you're going, you'll be lucky.'

'I knew you'd say something like that. I've noticed that, when you write, you can't resist the opportunity for a smart remark.'

'Why should I labour to be dull? Should I apologize for entertaining you?'

'Not if you *do* entertain me.'

'You smiled.'

'I was being polite.'

'For that you may ask another question.'

'I was going to. What do you look for in a book?'

'My place, or a misplaced train ticket.'

'There you go again. Can't resist the glib retort.'

'You asked for it. You should use words more carefully. Regard it as a lesson.'

'All right. I'm more obliging than you. What special qualities please you in a book?'

'Characters I care about; humour; distinction in writing . . .'

'In that order?'

'No. I think the way of telling comes first. A good actor can make more of a dull line than an amateur can make of Othello's farewell. But most of all I want a book to present me with a world I can live in.'

'Do you like rude books?'

'Not as much as you do.'

'Prude.'

'If you like. But I can't help it if I enjoy *Pride and Prejudice* more than *Fanny Hill*. I find rude books boring.'

'I find *Pride and Prejudice* boring.'

'So would any other grubby little brat . . .'

'You're losing your temper again.'

'Yes. And there's another lesson. You should care about a good book – care enough to become angry in its defence; even as you should grow warm in the defence of a friend maligned.'

'I hate history.'

'So what?'

'Aren't you going to get angry and leap to its defence?'

'Why should I?'

'As you always set your stories in the past, I would have thought you liked history.'

'I don't.'

'Why do you use it, then?'

'That's my affair.'

'Not when I've paid for this book. If you're not interested in history, why do you make such elaborate use of it?'

'I've been asked that before.'

'Big deal.'

'Oh well, let me answer your question this way – '

'You sound like a Party Political Broadcast. I want a straight answer.'

'There isn't one. I write fiction; I deal in lies. Whatever answer I give will be governed by the needs of narrative and illusion. Questions set up more than one answer . . . even as a theme in music suggests many variations. When Diabelli asked for a variation on his waltz, Beethoven could scarcely be confined to thirty-three.'

'Do you think you're Beethoven?'

*'Eh? What was that you said?'*

'I – Oh, what an awful joke! I do believe you arranged the whole thing for that feeble piece of comedy.'

'So what! If you knew how many stately edifices of prose had been erected to house one hopeful witticism (subsequently struck out), you would be horrified and, knowing the puritanism of the young, disgusted by the falsity of it all.'

'I'm getting disgusted by your failure to answer my question.'

'Oh yes. Why do I set my stories in the past? To be honest (or as honest as I can be) – '

'Must you keep using brackets?'

'Brackets keep up shelves – and shelves support books.'

'Why did I ask?'

'As I was saying, to be honest, I am that type of novelist who is an actor manqué. Like an actor I need pretence. I'm the sort of actor who, if he were appearing in a modern play, would not dream of appearing even in his own socks. I need all the trappings of illusion. I need to efface myself before I can be myself. I need to go away into another age before I can act out my fantasies . . .'

'Isn't that a sort of failure – a cowardice before the world of today?'

'Not entirely. I try to work by analogy. I rely on the phenomenon that the commonplace is rendered sharper by being placed in unexpected surroundings.'

'You said "not entirely". You admit, then, there's a little of the failure about it?'

'If I didn't think I'd failed before, I'd have precious little incentive to try again.'

'Why did you pick on the Eighteenth Century?'

'It suited me. Have you read Chesterton's *The Man who was Thursday*?'

'No.'

'A good book. There's a splendid passage near the end when all the characters appear in rather grand fancy dress. Each of them has instinctively chosen that costume that brings out his own inner nature to the most striking effect. Perhaps I chose the Eighteenth Century because, with increasing years, I felt the need of a wig? Doubtless, had I been blessed with long ears instead of diminishing hair, I would have written about rabbits.'

'I like that.'

'Thank you. I think I see a gleam of humanity in you.'

'So you are an actor-novelist – whatever that may be. Would you describe yourself as a method actor-novelist; or the other sort?'

'Let me answer you this way – '

'You ought to go in for politics.'

'Method-actor novelist. I try to approach my subject from within and work my way outwards. I can't abide that type of historical novel that superimposes an observer (usually an accident-prone boy) on a great event for no other purpose than to comment, with merciless detail, on things and people on whom he has no more effect than a boy of glass.'

'A bit vague; but I think I know what you mean. If you were to write about a great historical event, you would deal with the actual people who had an effect on it? Is that right?'

'Not exactly. I'd only write about an event that seemed to me to have some contemporary point; and far from touching too closely on actual historical figures, whose course is well known, I'd try to bring out of the shadows – ourselves.'

'Isn't that rather mis-using history?'

'On the contrary. It's using it. If history has any value beyond providing a livelihood for historians, it is to enlarge the imagination, to provide more acres for the mind to grow in. The humblest household plant, as it grows, needs to be transplanted into larger and larger vessels. With the shrinkage of space to live in, individual freedom becomes much more an inward affair. Though we may scarcely swing a cat in our cities, we may still swing a dinosaur in our minds.'

'Was that on the spur of the moment?'

'On the horn of a dilemma. I was trying to find a resounding end.'

'Are you hinting?'

'I am.'

'All right. Will you sign my autograph book?'

'I'd rather sign your copy of one of my own books.'

'I – er – haven't got any.'

'Haven't you read them, then?'

'Oh yes. But I don't *buy* them. I get them from the library.'

# II

# THIS FEAR OF DRAGONS
## Ursula Le Guin

M Y subject was to be Fantasy. But I have not been feeling very fanciful lately, and could not decide what to say; so I have been going about picking people's brains for ideas. 'What about fantasy? Tell me something about fantasy.' And one friend of mine said: 'All right, I'll tell you something fantastic. Ten years ago, I went to the children's room of the library of such-and-such a city, and asked for *The Hobbit*; and the librarian told me, "Oh, we keep that only in the adult collection; we don't feel that escapism is good for children."'

My friend and I had a good laugh and shudder over that, and we agreed that things have changed a great deal in these past ten years. That kind of moralistic censorship of works of fantasy is very uncommon now, in the children's libraries. But the fact that the children's libraries have become oases in the desert, doesn't mean that there isn't still a desert. The point of view from which that librarian spoke still exists. She was merely reflecting, in perfect good faith, something that goes very deep in the American character: a moral disapproval of fantasy, a disapproval so intense, and often so aggressive, that I cannot help but see it as arising, fundamentally, from fear.

So: Why are Americans afraid of dragons?

Before I try to answer my question, let me say that it isn't only Americans who are afraid of dragons. I suspect that almost all very highly technological peoples are more or less anti-fantasy. There are several national literatures which, like ours, have had no tradition of adult fantasy for the past several hundred years: the French, for instance. But then you have the Germans, who have a good deal; and the English, who have it, and love it, and do it better than anyone else. So this fear of dragons is not merely a Western, or a technological, phenomenon. But I do not want to get into these vast historical questions; I will speak of modern Americans, the only people I know well enough to talk about.

In wondering why Americans are afraid of dragons, I began to realize that a great many Americans are not only anti-fantasy, but altogether anti-fiction. We tend, as a people, to look upon all works of the imagination as suspect, or as contemptible.

'My wife reads novels. I haven't got the time.'

'I used to read that science fiction stuff when I was a teen-ager, but of course I don't now.'

'Fairy stories are for kids. I live in the real world.'

Who speaks so? Who is it that dismisses *War and Peace, The Time Machine*, and *A Midsummer Night's Dream* with this perfect self-assurance? It is, I fear, the man in the street—the hardworking, over-thirty American male – the men who run my country.

Such a rejection of the entire art of fiction is related to several American characteristics: our Puritanism, our work ethic, our profit-mindedness, and even our sexual mores.

To read *War and Peace* or *The Lord of the Rings* plainly is not 'work' – you do it for pleasure. And if it cannot be justified as 'educational' or as 'self-improvement', then, in the Puritan value system, it can only be self-indulgence or escapism. For pleasure is not a value to the Puritan; on the contrary, it is a sin.

Equally, in the businessman's value system, if an act does not bring in an immediate, tangible profit, it has no justification at all. Thus the only person who has an excuse to read Tolstoy or Tolkien is the English teacher, because he gets paid for it. But our businessman might allow himself to read a best-seller now and then; not because it is a good book, but because it is a best-seller – it is a success, it has made money. To the strangely mystical mind of the money-changer this justifies its existence; and by reading it he may participate, a little, in the power and *mana* of its success. If this is not magic, by the way, I don't know what it is.

The last element, the sexual one, is more complex. I hope I will not be understood as being sexist if I say that, within the American culture, I believe that this anti-fiction attitude is basically a male one. The American boy and man is very commonly forced to define his maleness by rejecting certain traits, certain human gifts and potentialities, which our culture defines as 'womanish' or 'childish'. And one of these traits or potentialities is, in cold sober fact, the absolutely essential human faculty of Imagination.

Having got this far, I went quickly to the dictionary.

The *Shorter Oxford Dictionary* says:

Imagination: 1. The action of imagining, or forming a mental concept of what is not actually present to the senses; 2. The mental consideration of actions or events not yet in existence.

Very well; I certainly can let 'absolutely essential human faculty' stand. But I must narrow the definition to fit our present subject. By Imagination, then, I personally mean the free play of the mind, both intellectual and sensory. By 'play' I mean recreation, re-creation, the recombination of what is known into what is new. By 'free' I mean that the action is done without an immediate object of profit – spontaneously. That does not mean, however, that there may not be a purpose behind the free play of the mind, a goal; and the goal may be a very serious object indeed. Children's imaginative play is clearly a practising at the acts and emotions of adulthood; a child who did not play would not become mature. As for the free play of an adult mind, its result may be *War and Peace*, or the Theory of Relativity.

To be free, after all, is not to be undisciplined. I should say that the discipline of the imagination may in fact be the essential method or technique of both art and science. It is our Puritanism, insisting that discipline means repression or punishment, which confuses the subject. To discipline something, in the proper sense of the word, does not mean to repress it, but to train it – to encourage it to grow, and act, and be fruitful, whether it is a peach tree or a human mind.

I think that a great many American men have been taught just the opposite. They have learned to repress their imagination, to reject it as something childish or effeminate, unprofitable, and probably sinful.

They have learned to fear it. But they have never learned to discipline it at all.

Now, I doubt that the imagination can be suppressed. If you truly eradicated it in a child, he would grow up to be an egg-plant. Like all our evil propensities, the imagination will out. But if it is rejected and despised, it will grow into wild and weedy shapes; it will be deformed. At its best it will be mere ego-centred daydreaming; at its worst it will be wishful thinking, which is a very dangerous occupation when it is taken seriously. Where literature is concerned, in the old, truly Puritan days, the only permitted reading was the Bible. Nowadays, with our secular Puritanism, the man who refuses to read novels because it's unmanly to do so, or because they aren't true, will most likely end up watching bloody detective thrillers on the television, or reading hack Westerns or sports stories, or going in for pornography, from *Playboy* on down. It is his starved imagination, craving nourishment, that forces him to do so. But he can rationalize such entertainment by saying that it is realistic – after all, sex exists, and there are criminals, and there are baseball players, and there used to be cowboys – and also by saying that it is virile, by which he means that it doesn't interest most women.

That all these genres are sterile, hopelessly sterile, is a reassurance to him, rather than a defect. If they were genuinely realistic, which is to say genuinely imagined and imaginative, he would be afraid of them. Fake realism is the escapist literature of our time. And probably the ultimate escapist reading is that masterpiece of total unreality, the daily Stock Market Report.

Now what about our man's wife? She probably wasn't required to squelch her private imagination in order to play her expected role in life, but she hasn't been trained to discipline it either. She is allowed to read novels, and even fantasies. But, lacking training and encouragement, her fancy is likely to glom on to very sickly fodder, such things as soap operas, and 'true romances', and nursey novels, and historico-sentimental novels, and all the rest of the baloney ground out to replace genuine imaginative works by the artistic sweatshops of a society which is profoundly distrustful of the uses of the imagination.

What, then, are the uses of the imagination?

You see, I think we have a terrible thing here: a hardworking, upright, responsible citizen, a full-grown, educated person, who is afraid of dragons, and afraid of hobbits, and scared to death of fairies. It's funny, but it's also terrible. Something has gone very wrong. I don't know what to do about it but to try and give an honest answer to that person's question, even though he often asks it in an aggressive and contemptuous tone of voice. 'What's the good of it all,' he says, 'dragons and hobbits and little green men – what's the *use* of it?' . . .

The truest answer, unfortunately, he won't even listen to. He won't hear it. The truest answer is, 'The use of it is to give you pleasure and delight.'

'I haven't got the time,' he snaps, swallowing a pill for his ulcer and rushing off to the golf course.

So we try the next-to-truest answer. It probably won't go down much better, but it must be said: 'The use of imaginative fiction is to deepen your understanding of your world, and your fellow men, and your own feelings, and your destiny.'

To which I fear he will retort, 'Look, I got a rise last year, and I'm giving my family the best of everything, we've got two cars and a colour TV. I understand enough of the world!'

And he is right, unanswerably right, if that is what he wants, and all he wants.

The kind of thing you learn from reading about the problems of a hobbit who is trying to drop a magic ring into an imaginary volcano has very little to do with your social status, or material success, or income. Indeed, if there is any relationship, it is a negative one. There is an inverse correlation between Fantasy and Money. That is a law, known to economists as Le Guin's Law. If you want a striking example of Le Guin's Law, just give a lift to one of those people along the roads who own nothing but a back pack, a guitar, a fine head of hair, a smile, and a thumb. Time and again, you will find that these waifs have read *The Lord of the Rings* – some of them can practically recite it. But now take Aristotle Onassis, or J. Paul Getty: could you believe that those men ever had anything to do, at any age, under any circumstances, with a hobbit?

But to carry my example a little further, and out of the realm of economics, did you ever notice how very gloomy Mr Onassis and Mr Getty and all those billionaires look, in their photographs? They have this strange, pinched look, as if they were hungry. As if they were hungry for something, as if they had lost something and were trying to think where it could be, or perhaps what it could be, what it was they've lost.

Could it be their childhood?

So I arrive at my personal defence of the uses of the imagination, especially in fiction, and most especially in fairy-tale, legend, fantasy, science fiction, and the rest of the lunatic fringe. To make that defence, as I did when I first put these thoughts together, before an audience of children's librarians was to bring coals to Newcastle: for the children's librarians I have met seem to be what they are and to do what they do just for this reason, that they have not denied their own childhood. They believe that maturity is not an outgrowing, but a growing up; that an adult is not a dead child, but a child who survived. They believe that all the best faculties of a mature human being exist in the child, and that if these faculties are encouraged in youth they will act well and wisely in the adult, but if they are repressed and denied in the child they will stunt and cripple the adult personality. And finally they believe that one of the most deeply human, and humane, of these faculties is the power of imagination; so that it is our pleasant duty, as librarians, or teachers, or parents, or writers, or simply as grownups, to encourage that faculty of imagination in our children, to encourage it to grow freely, to flourish like the green bay tree, by giving it the best, absolutely the best and purest, nourishment that it can absorb. And never, under any circumstances, to squelch it, or sneer at it, or imply that it is childish, or unmanly, or untrue.

For fantasy is true, of course. It isn't factual, but it is true. Children know that. Adults know it too, and that is precisely why many of them are afraid of fantasy. They know that its truth challenges, even threatens, all that is false, all that is phoney, unnecessary, and trivial in the life they have let themselves be forced into living. They are afraid of dragons, because they are afraid of freedom.

So I believe that we should trust our children. Normal children do not confuse reality and fantasy – they confuse them much less often than we adults do (as a certain great fantasist pointed out in a story called 'The Emperor's New Clothes'). Children know perfectly well that unicorns aren't real, but they also know that books about unicorns, if they are good books, are true books. All too often that's more than Mummy and Daddy know; for in denying their childhood, the adults have denied half their knowledge, and are left with the sad, sterile little fact: 'Unicorns aren't real.' And that fact is one that never got anybody anywhere (except in the story *The Unicorn in the Garden*, by another great fantasist, in which it is shown that a devotion to the unreality of unicorns may get you straight into the loony bin). It is by such statements as, 'Once upon a time there was a dragon' or 'In a hole in the ground there lived a hobbit', – it is by such beautiful non-facts that we fantastic human beings may arrive, in our peculiar fashion, at the truth.

# 12

# LOST SUMMER

## *Rosemary Sutcliff*

ONE of our foremost writers (it might have been George Bernard Shaw, but I don't think it was) once said that he disliked writing only one degree less than he disliked not writing. That, of course, is an overstatement, but I suspect that there's a hideous grain of truth in it.

Writing is much too much like gruellingly hard work, even though it is work one loves.

I suppose most writers know the joy once, perhaps twice, in their whole working life, of a book which almost creates itself, 'as a bird sings'. Only the very fortunate know it more than twice. The first time comes, almost always, and for obvious reasons, with the first book. We plunge into it so light-heartedly, so eagerly. We have not the remotest idea of the sheer hard work, the problems and difficulties and heartbreaks involved in creative writing; and so the book is a delight. Quite often it is slightly illicit, being written in time snatched from other things that we really ought to be doing instead, such as our proper jobs, or sleeping, or getting healthy exercise; and this, of course, gives an added joy to the enterprise. The second book, supposing that the first has found a publisher, is a very different matter, written with a good deal of anxiety as to whether we can 'do it again'. If we get past that, there may be another book, somewhere among the next four or so, that will come in the same almost magical way as the first. But it's only the truly blessed among us, or those who have the luck of Old Nick, who find the joy of such a book again, after our list of titles has reached five or six. By that time we are too well aware of the strains and stresses, the problems, the dark patches when nothing will come, and the fear that nothing will ever come again. We still love writing, it's the breath of life to us, even on the days when nothing comes right and we think how nice it would be to be a bus conductor or stockbroker or an old man's darling and never have to write another *word*. Speaking personally, if for some reason I am unable to write for a while I develop spiritual constipation. But as the years go by,

I become more and more of a perfectionist, and spend more and more time sitting and staring at a blank page and wondering exactly how to put down the thing that I am trying to say, instead of happily scribbling whatever comes into my head, with the proviso that if it isn't right, I can always go over it again later and make all well.

For me, there have been two, among my published books, written with this effortless delight. The first was *The Queen Elizabeth Story*. I had already written *The Chronicles of Robin Hood*, but that was a re-telling, an adopted child, while the *Q.E.S.* was the first book born out of my own being. The other was *The Eagle of the Ninth*. I hope and think that I have written better books since; but *Eagle*, with this quality of specialness, of delight, of coming as a bird sings, remains my best-beloved among my own books, and – presumably something of all this passes through the writing, to reach out to the reader on the far side – it still seems to be the most generally popular with children, too.

But oh! how I wish I still had my very first book of all: written some time in the second half of the War; never submitted to a publisher, never even typed, never read by anybody in all the world except me.

It was called Summer Something, or Something Summer. I have forgotten the exact name; but almost everything else about it I remember vividly and with a kind of bloom on the memory much like the bloom on the memory of first love. In writing it, I don't think I ever stopped to wonder whether it was supposed to be for adults or children; it was just the story I wanted to write, the book of my heart. It was set in the eighteenth century, which was odd, because I have always claimed that I can't handle anything later than the Civil War: that if I try, it turns to Cloak-and-Dagger on me. This was certainly not Cloak-and-Dagger; it was a very simple and quiet story, tracing a few months in the life of Jane-Anne, aged eleven and sent, while her mother recovered from a miscarriage, to spend the summer with a strict Great Aunt in Exeter. She escapes from the chill correctitude of her aunt's household, to the warmth and refuge of the local doctor's bachelor establishment next door, where the doctor's ex-soldier son was slowly recovering from a wound received at Minden. (Yes, of course, if there seems anything familiar about this, a good deal of it found its way years later, or sixteen hundred years earlier, whichever way you like to look at it, into the Summer which Marcus spent convalescing with Uncle Aquila, in *The Eagle of the Ninth*. Even the rescue operation carried out, under protest, by the older man, even the second probing of the young man's wound.) Looking back, I realize that the whole thing was heavily derivative, with strong overtones of Elizabeth Goudge, whom I had lately discovered, and a card party, given by Great Aunt, which, with its candles on the table and the monstrous nid-nodding shadows of mob caps on the parlour walls behind the players, was pure unadulterated *Cranford*.

It was a story in which very little moved, except the slowly developing relationship between the young man and the little girl, each meeting the other's need in that particular period in their lives, against the setting of a big untidy garden flowering its way from Spring through Summer into early Autumn. I know every smallest thing about that garden still: the amber velvet bees booming in the lime tree, the flaming poppies with the soot-spill of blue-black pollen in their throats, the apple trees at the foot of the garden, just coming into blossom when Jane-Anne first entered it.

There was a dog, of course: two in fact. One a flesh-and-blood dog, large and shaggy and kind; the other a china greyhound couchant and cross-pawed on the lid of a pale green trinket-box, Jane-Anne's most treasured possession, which she dropped down the well at the bottom of Great Aunt's very different garden, for a sacrifice, to reinforce her prayers that God would 'Make It All Right' for Hugh, undergoing that second probing of the wound.

There was absolutely everything that I wanted to put into that story. I knew nothing about the self-discipline required in a writer. I scattered delights on every page, and found, in doing so, the same kind of escape, refuge, what you will, from a very lonely girlhood (I must have been about twenty, but I think I was young for my age) that I had accorded to my small heroine.

And in the end it got out of hand and went wrong, because I had not the experience, either of life or writing, to know that it was an idyll, a Summer fragment that reached its natural end when, with the apples ripening on the trees at the bottom of the garden, Jane-Anne departed back her family and Hugh set off to walk the wards of a big London hospital and train to be a doctor like his father. I tried to carry on through a second half that refused to come to life, to a conventional Happy Ever After ending that had no true place in the story. And because it would not work out, I thought simply that it was destined to remain unfinished – and put it away in a drawer, but never forgot about it.

Later, echoes of it, lingering around my mind, found their way into other books, notably into that Summer in *The Eagle of the Ninth*. Later still, when my father and I moved from Devon to Sussex, I found the old manuscript, and consigned it, along with quite a few other things that I have since regretted, to the bonfire.

I wish so much I had not. It was the first story I ever wrote, and despite all its faults, I began learning my trade in the writing of it; and no book since has ever given me quite the joy that it gave me.

Remembering it in as much detail as I do, I could probably re-write it now; make, as it were, a reconstruction. But it would not be the real thing. Perhaps you have to be twenty, and young for your age, to write that particular real thing.

# 13

# POETRY MOSAIC:
## SOME REFLECTIONS ON
## WRITING VERSE FOR CHILDREN

*Ian Serraillier*

A FEW years ago *Only Connect*, a symposium of Readings on Children's Literature, was published by the Oxford University Press. I was surprised to find that its 471 pages included nothing about verse written for children. The editors, in their search for 'insight and informed contemporary thinking', could apparently find nothing significant on this area of the subject. It is one on which critics are often hesitant to commit themselves. I don't intend to try to fill the gap now, but merely to offer some observations of my own, in the light of personal experience, present opportunities and pointers to the future.

Obviously the children's poet must reflect both the real and the imaginative world of childhood. But where does he differ from the poet who writes for adults? In *From Two to Five*, translated and edited by Miriam Morton, University of California Press 1968, the Russian poet Kornei Chukovsky made a list of 'commandments for children's poets'. These are largely concerned with technique. As young children think in images, the poem (he says) must be graphic, with each verse – or even each couplet – suggesting to the artist a suitable illustration. Not only does he regard illustration as essential at this stage, but rhyme too, for rhyme helps the young child to remember more easily, and also to get the sense. The poet must choose his rhyme words carefully, for they must be the main carriers of the meaning. If the gist of the story is not clear from the rhymes alone, then they must be changed. Though I have myself written little for the very youngest, I feel that there is much good sense in Chukovsky's advice. Older children, he goes on to say, will expect more advanced stylistic standards. There must be a gradual progress towards bringing them within reach of adults' thoughts and perceptions – and within reach, too, of the wider world of poetry, especially that of the past.

Folk poetry is one field with obvious attractions for children. The

English and Scottish ballads are usually recognized as 'the richest body of popular poetry in the world'. Apart from a few dozen well-known examples, children meet the rest (if they meet them at all) only in prose retellings, usually padded out with tiresome historical detail. The lyric quality and the rapid story-telling of the originals, in which so much is left to the imagination, go for nothing. There must be other ways of preserving their flavour, and who is better equipped to tackle the problems than the poet?

The folk poetry of other countries is another source, which has only been partially explored. This brings in the linguist and translator. But the paradox is that a poem cannot be properly translated; it must be recreated, so that it sounds fresh and spontaneous, as if it really belongs to its new tongue. The expert linguist is rarely the best person to tackle this. A poet with only a limited knowledge of the foreign language is likely to be more successful; better still if the poet and linguist can join forces, as C. Day Lewis and Mátyás Sárközi have done in a recent translation of traditional Hungarian rhymes, *The Tomtit in The Rain* (Chatto & Windus, 1971). I have myself had a go at some of the heroic folk poetry of Serbia, composed by anonymous minstrels during the long years of Turkish oppression that followed the nation's defeat at Kossovo in 1389. Their ballads, passed like our own from generation to generation by word of mouth, helped to keep up the people's spirits and make their suffering bearable. Their particular hero was Prince Marko, a kind of Serbian Robin Hood, as sympathetic to the poor and oppressed, but fiercer and more aggressively defiant, yet at the same time tenderly devoted to his mother, to his wonder horse Sharatz, and to all birds and animals. I had only a scholar's literal line by line translation of the original seventeenth-century texts to work from, and my own versions of the ballads can at best be only faint echoes of the vigorous voices of those unknown story tellers of the past.

I am always conscious of my own linguistic limitations. In some older cultures a poet had to be specially trained in his craft and was not recognized until he had satisfied high professional standards. Today he must learn his craft as he goes along. In his essay 'The Poet and the City' W. H. Auden has prescribed what he regarded as the ideal education for a modern poet. In his 'day-dream College of Bards', as he called it, he would put first on the curriculum 'in addition to English, at least one ancient language, probably Greek or Hebrew, and two modern languages'. But real schools fall short of this ideal. I was brought up on a solid diet of Latin and Greek, seasoned with a sprinkling of French and a pinch of English. In those days a classical education was the thing; English, if taught at all, was a left-over job that any mutt could tackle. Besides being made to learn my irregular verbs by heart, I had to translate, construe and compose in classical languages. I was even taught how to write poems in Latin and Greek – but never in English, as many children are rightly encouraged to do today, when little Latin and hardly any Greek (the more poetic language) survive. Those wrestling matches with hexameters and pentameters at the age of fourteen or fifteen may have been a harsh discipline, but it has served me well and I have more gratitude than regret. But after Honour Mods. at Oxford I decided I had had enough of the classics, and I opted for Finals in English Language and Literature. It was a true awakening. After the classical grind, even Anglo-Saxon and Middle English held few terrors.

Perhaps this early initiation into the basic structure of language made it easier for me to turn more recently to a fresh field, the writing of verse for young overseas readers for whom English is a foreign language. As far as I know, this approach has not been tried before. This old nonsense rhyme is familiar to many English children from an early age:

> Three children sliding on the ice
> Upon a summer's day,
> It so fell out they all fell in;
> The rest, they ran away.
>
> Now had these children stayed at home
> Or slid upon dry ground,
> Ten thousand pounds to one penny
> They had not all been drowned.
>
> You parents all, that children have,
> (And you that have got none,)
> If you would have them safe abroad,
> Pray keep them safe at home.

Easy, you might think – but a South American or West German thirteen-year-old in his second year of learning English would find the structure difficult and the sentiments childish. The problem for the writer trying to reach these readers is how to express more sophisticated concepts and contemporary subject matter in simple vocabulary and syntax, without the result sounding watered down or contrived. Not an easy task, but I have found it stimulating and challenging.

Another challenge is the commissioned poem. There is, I think, a general feeling that poems are begotten of inspiration only and cannot be produced to order. But if stories, plays, operas, symphonies and ballets can be commissioned, why not poems too? A sense of purpose can often supply the inspiration needed. A year or two ago *Merry-go-round*, the BBC Schools television programme for seven- to nine-year-olds, did a series on Roman Britain. I was asked to contribute a poem about a mosaic, and I chose as my subject the dolphin mosaic at Fishbourne Roman Palace, Chichester. A class of children at a local primary school was watching the series. They paid a visit to the palace and I went with them. I even made an eight-millimetre ciné film of the outing, to show to their Parent-Teachers' Association. It was hardly a rival to the film the BBC made, but it got by all right with the PTA. They were intrigued to watch their children making themselves at home among the splendours of an ancient Roman palace. Here is the poem I wrote:

### DOLPHIN MOSAIC

A Roman craftsman made this floor,
This stone mosaic picture – shells, vases,
Wild creatures bounding through a summer sea.
He sat the boy astride a dolphin's back,
Trident in hand, with wings to steady him;
He made twin horses, to gallop the waves with wings;
Twin panthers too, with tails and prancing paws;
And last, on the leafy border, a lonely bird.

The craftsman sighed when his joyful work was done.
'I'm tired,' he said, 'of this wet and shivering land.
Tomorrow I sail for home.' Then Roman families came;
They walked on the square sea, they lay on couches
To dine and drink; the little grandson of the house
Fell sprawling on the floor and broke his goblet.
After a hundred years, a cry of, 'Fire!
The palace is ablaze from end to end!'
A cloud of smoke, drips of molten lead,
Falling tiles and nails and window glass,
And rafters shooting flame . . . Slowly,
Through centuries of silence, the earth surged in,
Hiding the picture from the ploughman's sight.

Then someone shouted, 'The trench for the water-main –
We'll dig it here!' A noise of engines,
Then the digging stopped. Careful fingers
Scraped the earth away; astonished eyes
Gazed at the dolphin boy, the stony sea,
The horses and the panthers, and at last,
There in the leafy border, the lonely bird.

My aim was to tell the story behind the mosaic and its discovery in the 1960s, to get the children to feel something of the creative inspiration that went into its making, and to provide a rough camera script as well. Ambitious perhaps, but as a poem requires a concentration of language that prose less readily commands, I feel it was the right medium here. It was beautifully spoken and the BBC film combination of close-ups of the mosaic with an artist's drawings of the action was a most effective accompaniment. After watching the programme, the children made their own mosaic – a life-size mermaid – from hundreds of small paper squares cut out of the Sunday colour supplements. It was displayed on the classroom wall for the rest of that term.

The use of a poem to illustrate some aspect of a wider theme, with or without practical application in the classroom, is suitable for a variety of subjects. For a BBC TV programme for six-year-olds about weaving I have made a puppet play in verse of Hans Andersen's story, *The Emperor's New Clothes*. This could also be spoken and acted by children themselves. But perhaps my most exciting venture of all was the work I undertook for John Hosier of the BBC TV Schools Music department. The commission was to write with a composer a story in verse and song that children could sing, speak and perform themselves, using percussion instruments. The final work would last about twenty-five minutes, but the whole piece was to be taught in eight weekly programmes throughout the term. A class of children from a school in the London area learnt the work in advance, and the baritone John Langstaff came over from Washington to conduct them in the studio and, with their assistance, to teach the work to viewing classes. I did this on three occasions altogether, basing the libretto on a folk tale from three different countries, whose civilization the children were encouraged to explore for themselves in a variety of ways. For *The Midnight Thief*, a tale from Mexico, I collaborated with Richard Rodney Bennett; for *Ahmet the Woodseller* (from Somalia) with Gordon Crosse; and for *The Turtle Drum* (from Japan) with Malcolm

Arnold. To work with these composers, and sometimes with children and producers too, was for me a new and enriching experience, a welcome opportunity to venture away from my self-indulgent typewriter into a wider world, where ideas had to be tested and made to function.

All art forms, if they are to survive, must adapt to new conditions, and poetry is no exception. If, as my experience suggests, this is to mean some measure of escape from the printed page, that is no bad thing: it may again come closer to its origins – in song and dance and the spoken word. The radio poet writes to be listened to, not to be read. In television he has not been used as much as he could be, though poets such as John Betjeman and Ted Hughes have pointed the way to what should, with a little enterprise, be a promising future. As for the children's poet, he too has a role to play, a wider one than in the past. If he's still around in the distant future, whatever the outward changes, he will probably still be a curious mixture of creator, interpreter and craftsman.

# 14

# DISCOVERING THE PATTERN
## *Penelope Farmer*

WRITING fiction is for me an escape from all kinds of things I dislike and am bad at – abstractions, for instance, and verbal reasoning. I've always been better at images than arguments – to the despair of anyone who tried to teach me at university. Not only that, I like the seeming anonymity – the way you can hide behind your characters, and never admit anything outright. Unfortunately, though, if you write fiction with any degree of success there comes a point where people start asking you questions about it: why, how, so on, so forth. Indeed, what motivates writers seems perennially fascinating – why else this essay? Why else this book? Which brings me back, full circle, to all the things I had so thankfully abandoned: statement, reason, argument. Of course, I do not have to answer the questions if I don't want to. But in a little while, whether I like it or not, they begin to intrigue me; to the extent that lately I've been brooding on them a great deal, though I'm not sure that's a good thing. And it brings me ultimately to . . . what? Form, I suppose. I find I have become obsessed by the idea of form: which means that I shall have to write about it here. The problem is that the subject is so complex. I am in such confusion about it, I hardly know where to begin. I cannot define it, for a start; probably because as an abstraction I find it meaningless, form for me only existing where I can see, feel, respond to it, whether within nature or some human artefact. I know that it is everywhere in the natural world on a far larger and wider scale than we used to suspect, or can now comprehend: stars beyond stars, atoms within atoms, to infinity. I would guess that this omnipresence is the reason we seem to need, crave form, to create it or to find it. But I cannot analyse form in nature because I dropped biology at the age of thirteen, so am no scientist. Nor can I easily analyse it in art, either: because the more perfect art is, the harder it is to work out why. Recently, for my own purpose, I have been picking away at stories by Jean Rhys – some of them perfect of their kind, I think. But that very perfection makes them like seamless garments – impossible to dissect, let alone use as models for other garments – stories.

I cannot, as you see, keep myself out of this (though writing essays at school you were always told to; which perhaps explains the educated Englishman's continual bashful use of 'one' when actually he means 'I'). Since my own interest in form is necessarily technical in part, and has a strong literary bias, subjectivity does conveniently set limits to an otherwise infinite subject; – means I can define form in two fairly simple senses, at least. First, in the sense of genre – poetry, for instance, as against the novel – each form with its own subsections, such as the lyric and the epic poem, the realistic or the comic novel, the gothick or the fantasy. Second, as the structure of any particular work – successful or not – and within that structure the varied patternings, emotional or social, or merely technical, large or small, internal or external, that go to compose it. But it is not quite as simple as that. The printed page may be one place where you can look for and find form – or its lack – but the matter neither starts nor ends there, you cannot just leave it on that page, or expect to distil it from another; not if you are a writer, anyway. It relates to a whole pattern of living and being; of ways of observation, and ways of feeling; is discovered perhaps, in the end result, rather than invented. Anthony Powell, for instance, certainly did not invent the social patternings of his *Dance to the Music of Time*: the way, as time passes, its characters meet, separate, regroup, remeet, re-separate. The pattern may seem arbitrary and contrived at a first reading – but all at once you begin to notice similar patternings in your own life. They were always there, only you had never defined them, till Powell did it for you, and rather differently, Proust, before him.

But then, why Powell? Why did he discover this aspect rather than another? What makes him write formal, comic, highly-polished novels, observing relationships in social rather than emotional context? While Iris Murdoch, say, writes her very different kind of novels combining, rather curiously, convoluted, and sometimes sensationalist, emotional relationships, with deep philosophical questionings. Why do they not write differently? The answers would probably boil down to pretty much the same as mine – on my considerably less exalted level – when I am asked why, as a writer for children, I do not produce nice, solid, useful novels on the problems of the adopted child or aimed at the reluctant reader, and so forth, instead of highly symbolic (according to some reviewers) obscure (according to others) – anyway, *difficult* fantasies. Very simply because I cannot. It is the same for everyone – no one can express himself effectively except in ways and forms suited to him. Too bad if the form happens to be unfashionable, too new or too old for others to recognize or accept. Either way it explains plenty of artists *manqués*: explains also the persistent geniuses, who remain unnoticed, till many years after they are dead; Blake the most striking of them all.

It is when you begin to explore new forms that you really become aware of this; and wonder perhaps what it means. Not immediately, since any new structuring cannot be understood and controlled at once. But ultimately, if you go on failing. It is partly a very simple matter of form and content having to be compatible – you cannot, for example, make a satisfactory story for seven-year-olds out of an idea strong enough to sustain an adult novel. But it is not just that; form and content may be compatible, but if neither is right for the writer, that will not help him. Some may reach a degree of competence even so, though their work lacks a spark it shows elsewhere. But others (me, for instance) cease in such circumstances to have any facility at all. I know that when I try to write stories within Jean Rhys's area, or Philippa Pearce's for that matter, I lose the simplest verbal competence; words become leaden, coagulate, I cannot write from page to page, let alone create a beginning, a middle and an end. Whereas writing within my usual form, fantasy, given time and given a good idea, I feel sometimes a kind of fluency and ease. And as for form, I scarcely have to look for it. I am aware of problems from time to time, make adjustments accordingly. But fundamentally I never impose it in any way. It pushes up from some unknown part of my mind, I can feel it happening, watch it slowly, gradually, fall neatly into place.

It seems that I need symbols and images; symbols being formalized, ritualized, often universal images – the sun, for instance, or the dark, or the power of flight. Since I have very few ideas indeed – envying the prolific, more extrovert fantasists, like Joan Aiken – I have to nurture each one carefully, squeeze it to the uttermost (digging very deeply into myself in the process, though often unaware of that), and letting it develop as it always must via images. Without those images, I cannot frame my idea and expand it into narrative.

For while poetry uses images straight, more or less, and usually very compressed, fantasy marches head-on into them. People actually fly, move about in time, swop identities; inanimate objects become animate and so on. For me the extraordinary is a means of looking at people sideways and finding out more about them – and me. But looking straight at them, at real instead of imagined life, I feel eyeless and earless; I can see, hear, describe, precisely nothing. Equally, without the symbols and the images they give me, I can find no form or structure anywhere. It was not till I came across the Celtic tree alphabets and calendars, took the tree for one central symbol, that I found a framework for my last book, *A Castle of Bone*, and was able to set about writing it.

But symbols jump uncannily, in ways you do not expect; because they touch echoes in yourself, I suppose, even if you do not know what they may stand for. I have had till now a very literal mind, and in *A Castle of Bone* at least two of them pursued me, rather than the other way about. The castle itself I took from a Welsh triad – only there it was a bone fortress. It did not seem relevant at all when I met it first; but as an image it would not leave me alone, wormed its way into the plot, relentlessly; until it became central. Yet I never thought of it as an image for man till I reached the last chapter (and never knew, either, that the Anglo-Saxon kenning for a man was a bone house). Even stranger was the old man in the story. I saw him mainly as a *deus-ex-machina*; certainly not as someone suggested later, as Tiresias, the blind seer, who explains the world in riddles for our own deciphering. And yet, every time he appeared, I referred carefully to the blind bust in the shop: even, eventually, giving it the old man's face. I find this alarming. A child wrote to me recently; 'I don't really like your books but I can't help reading them . . . *The Castle of Bone* . . . gave me a funny feeling.' Well, it gave and gives me some pretty funny feelings too.

Symbolism as unconscious as this makes for blind writing in a way. It is like walking along a tunnel in the dark, knowing the walls to be intricately patterned, occasionally, briefly, catching a glimpse of them, but mostly only sensing their presence, taking forms from them intuitively. But the tunnel must come to an end eventually, must be about to end perhaps, when you begin to recognize the symbols as they appear; and then, presumably, you burst out into the light. But what happens then, I do not know.

Since form is so personal, perhaps it is at this stage that you become so aware of it; when, suddenly, everything around you, every area of life, seems to develop a patterning, whether social ones, such as Powell dissects, or the emotional ones of an Iris Murdoch. It is a stage when almost everything you read and see and think seems to interconnect in the most unexpected ways (interests as diverse as Blake and wrestling, becoming for instance, logically compatible); when you find yourself quite coincidentally chasing the same theme through book after book, whether heavy fiction or detective stories, when you are drawn to books, or whatever, again apparently by coincidence, exactly when you need them, when they become relevant. Even writing this article, I began Hermann Hesse's *Narziss and Goldmund* (Hesse having wholly defeated me till now), became totally involved, and found myself reading this:

. . . those luckless artificers who, though they bear within them the highest gifts, can find no right craft by which to express them. There are many such who, seeing all the beauty of earth, can find no way to give it forth again, and share with others what they have seen.

And again two days later, even more relevantly, this:

. . . The pattern of any good image is no real, living form, or shape, although such shapes may have prompted the maker to it. Their true first pattern is not in flesh and blood, but in the mind. Such images have their home in the craftsman's soul.

It's very exhilarating in a way. But it means reading, seeing; perception of all kinds tends to become, perhaps dangerously, less a process of appreciation than a kind of personal decoding of symbols and ideas. And what effect does that have on writing, on discovery and creation of form? Is it ultimately destructive? Or does it lead on towards new tunnels, areas of darkness, with new hidden patternings to sense and to explore? Or how? Or what?

I only wish I knew.

# 15

# ANCIENT AND MODERN AND
# INCORRIGIBLY PLURAL

*Helen Cresswell*

World is suddener than we fancy it
World is crazier and more of it than we think
Incorrigibly plural. I peel and portion
A tangerine and spit the pips and feel
The drunkenness of things being various.

LOUIS MACNEICE

WHENEVER I am called upon to write or talk about why and how I write, I usually find myself using not my own, but other people's words. I quote endlessly – Gide, Russell, Blake, Lichtenberg, Manley Hopkins, Goethe, MacNeice . . . I have even had it recently suggested to me that I should publish a *Helen Cresswell Commonplace Book,* so it now looks as if people are beginning to notice. In fact it was this suggestion that made *me* notice, and having noticed, think about it.

I think there is more than one reason why I always quote other people about the writing process. Firstly, it is because I have an instinctive fear of meddling with my own inner mechanisms. I shall quote my (earlier) self on this:

These days we have a good many impressive terms for magic, all running into polysyllables and having a pleasantly authoritative ring to them. And these terms are all quite valid, and very useful to the psychologist himself and even to the critic. But to the creative writer they spell death – death to magic. The moment a writer becomes aware of his own creative processes, the moment he stands outside them and they become conscious, then they lose their dynamism, and he may as well lay down his pen. He who attempts to analyse magic while at the same time practising it stands in peril of finding symbol turn to cliché, intuition to conscious will, organic growth to mere plotting.*

I stand by this, adding only to clarify my point the analogy of the havoc that can be caused by paying attention to, say, one's own heartbeat.

* *Play,* Vol. 1, No. 1, September 1969.

Secondly, having all my life been a solitary and dedicated thinker, a muser, an amateur philosopher, I am always delighted whenever I come across an endorsement of my own beliefs from a superior mind. I then quote to give them added weight for myself, as well as for others.

But the third, and I suspect the real reason, is that whatever I have to say that is of any value whatever, is contained in my work itself. If I could say what I have to say in any other form, then I would do so. And in any case, I do not usually know what I *do* think until I have said it. *The Nightwatchmen* is, quite simply, the book of that title, every single word of it (hopefully). I could add that it is a book about individual freedom and, in particular, freedom of the imagination. I could describe how months after the book was published I suddenly recalled a recurrent childhood nightmare, the climax of which was my finding myself enclosed in an underground cavern and seeing, there in the gloom, a pair of green eyes. This certainly explains why I should have chosen Greeneyes as a symbol of threat, rather than giants or phantoms or blind men. It also throws a light on the part played in fantasy by the subconscious. But it does not really add anything at all to the *book*. *The Nightwatchmen* is *The Nightwatchmen* is *The Nightwatchmen*.

I do not make a habit of thinking about why I write for children. Any thoughts I have had at all on the matter have been a result of a direct question put to me by someone else. The last time I had to give an answer to it in print, this is what I wrote:

If you are going to use words (and I have no choice) you have to say something, and gradually you come to find that when you are saying what you really mean you tend to use words best of all, and so it is worth while finding out what you really mean. I am still working on this. With any luck, I shall *never* really be quite sure what I mean, and so I will never have to stop using words in order to find out. I think that may be one reason why my books are for children. They never know for sure what they mean, either. Most adults do. Most adults manage to find an attitude, and when they have found it, it takes them over, and fixes them like a fly in aspic (or whatever the expression is – I'm sure that's not it. Wasp in alabaster? Bee in marble? Fly in ointment. . . ? Drop it . . .)

Last night in bed I was reading Keats' letters for the first time for years. Just before I went to sleep I came across the letter in which he talks about 'negative capability'. This is a phrase indelibly fixed in my mind (like a fly in clover?) from school days, but I had quite forgotten what it meant. (If, indeed, I ever knew.) A week ago, if you had offered me a five pound note to tell you what 'negative capability' meant, I could not have told you. Which is extraordinary. Because it is exactly what *I* mean, exactly how I feel, exactly how I am as certain as so uncertain a person can be I shall always feel. It is:

'. . . when a man is capable of being in uncertainties, mysteries, doubts, without any irritable reaching after facts and reason.'

I might have known it meant that, or something like it. Keats was never the man to confuse truth with fact.*

This still stands, as it has always stood, ever since I began writing as a child. And it leads on to other thoughts I have had about my own work, again prompted by others, not myself. I am by now used to reading, every so often, that my work is 'old-fashioned', that its action takes place in an 'idealized rural England of the past', that it is not, in a word, contemporary.

This is the first time I have publicly challenged this view of what I write, and I do so now not in self defence (because I am not even sure whether this is meant as a charge) but in the interests of truthfulness.

I am amazed, even astounded, that my work does not seem modern to some people, because since I have given this matter any thought at all, it seems to me that it is not only contemporary in outlook but positively *avant garde*. So much so, that half the time people do not know what I am getting at. Recently I was speaking to an interviewer about Jung's Theory of Synchronicity, Kammerer's Law of Seriality and Arthur Koestler's *The Roots of Coincidence*. This came out in her article as: 'Helen Cresswell is a great believer in fate, and in the stars.' Which is not quite how I would have put it.

I did not know until I read Theodore Roszak's book *The Makings of a Counter Culture* a couple of years ago, that there *was* a counter culture. But I am delighted to find that there is (though there are very few signs of it where *I* live) and that I belong to it, and have done so all my life. In fact I must have been an unwitting founder member.

What this means, in a nutshell, is that I find the present technocracy alien and humanly barren, and that I do not believe in the one-sided development of rationality at the expense of every other aspect of human experience. I look for balance to the shadow side of the psyche, the subjective reality of the individual, the power of the creative imagination. I believe (and I *will* quote Blake):

The imagination is the only real and eternal world, of which our vegetable world is put a pale shadow.

* *Books for Your Children*, Vol. 16, No. 4.

I believe (and I *will* quote Lichtenberg):

If an angel were to tell us something of his philosophy, I do believe some of his propositions would sound like $2 \times 2 = 13$.

On the title-page of *The Bongleweed* (true to form) I quote Turgenev:

Whatever man prays for, he prays for a miracle. Every prayer reduces itself to this: 'Great God, grant that twice two be not four.'

Now I did not come across this statement and then write a book about it. I found it while the book was already with the printers, and had it inserted. Because by then, about a year after *The Bongleweed* was finished, I was fairly sure what it was about. I did not know when I started it. I never do. Pinned on the wall before me as I sit here now are some words of Leo Rosten: 'When you don't know where a road leads, it sure as hell will take you there.'

And these words say practically everything there is to be said about my writing processes. My books are roads, journeys, explorations. I do not know where I am going until I arrive there. I simply set out. I write at the top of a blank sheet the title I have given myself, and set out.

This is not properly expressed, and I never can find the right words to say it (probably because I do not really wish to.) When I was trying to say it recently to someone who was asking me questions, she said, 'You mean that your books are riddles that you set yourself, and you write them in order to solve them.' Which is more or less right, and here I am quoting other people's words again.

*The Bongleweed* probably comes as near to being a credo as anything I have yet written, though, of course, it is only my *latest* credo, as *The Nightwatchmen*, *The Beachcombers* and so on were in their turn. Each book simply rounds another bend in the road. And the more I read of writers like Jung, Koestler, Roszak, Wilson, Laing and Lyall Watson, the more I see that the road I am travelling is not one that has already been mapped, because it is one for which each traveller must make his *own* map. It is not a wistful, nostalgic tour with an already certain destination, but a *real* one, being travelled here and now by countless thousands of others (most of them young) and with no fixed point of arrival. There never can be a final destination because the meaning of the journey lies in the making of it. In a sense, the moment one sets out, one is there.

The Outlanders do not wear modern dress, but the journey they make from the safe confines of the familiar and definable to the uncharted places of the Outlands, is an inner one which people always have made and are still making. Recently I started Transcendental Meditation (which I am recommending to all my friends). The young graduate who instructed me had read this book, and pointed out that it might have been an allegory based on the experience of T.M., even to the detail of the Rhymers being finally given a secret word (a mantra) as a kind of key to themselves. He was right. But when I wrote *The Outlanders* seven or eight years ago, I had never heard of Transcendental Meditation. When I wrote that book I set out myself, with the Rhymers, and like them very nearly did not come back.

*The Beachcombers*, on the other hand, is a kind of balancing act between the two worlds of Blake – the pale 'vegetable world' of the Scavengers, and the 'real and eternal' one of the Beachcombers. The reason why this book has no ending, is because there *is* no ending – not a truthful one, at any rate. We are all of us caught in the tension between these two worlds. It is the very essence of the human condition, and the dilemma is one that is never ending, it lasts a whole life long. Decisions like these cannot be made once and for all. They must be renewed, almost hour by hour, and are subject to flux like the tides themselves. That is why Ned is left poised in anguish on the edge of decision:

How could he have decided to go, I ask myself – left his mother, home, friends, cast anchor and left the whole world behind? But then, I ask myself, how could he have stayed? How gone down to that empty beach before dawn and watched the Beachcombers sail into the breaking sky with their treasure? How gone back to that basement, and the Pickerings and Mr Blagger? It is unthinkable.

He will be poised there forever, and so are we all. Ned is certain of only one thing, and that is that treasure, if treasure there be, is for Beachcombers, not Scavengers. He hardly needs the Captain to tell him so: '"Treasure's not for Scavengers. Treasure's not that easy to come by. It's for them that watches, and works, and waits."'

But the world of the Scavengers is in a sense often more 'real' than that of the Beachcombers, it is the world of ticking clocks and grubbing for money and 'knowing what's what'. Ned himself recognizes this, even while preferring the life of the Beachcombers, and towards the end of the story finds himself almost submerged once and for all:

It was as if he were held in a spell and the spell was to do with darkness and to do with Mr Blagger and the turning of the cards and the relentless clock, and the spell was a spell that stopped all movement dead in its flight, that held everything frozen, powerless to move. It was as though life itself were trapped as if by the shutter of a camera, the whole world reduced to a negative.

Mr Blagger, Chief Scavenger, is the personification of what is sterile, fixed, uncreative. He plays patience, the very essence of time-wasting and passivity, to the iron ticking of the clock. And Ned, to escape, has to deny the reality of this even though it is before his very eyes. He has to assert his belief in the Beachcombers and make a blind act of faith, even though he has come to the point where he can no longer visualize the *Sea Queen* or even the sea. And when he does so, with enormous effort, he is rewarded by a renewal of certainty in that other reality:

When he mounted the ridge of dunes and looked down into the blindingly wet and gleaming bay he saw the Dallakers in a little group, beards and hair streaming, their bones shining through their wind-flattened rags, being *played* on.

'Jubilee!' he said, under his breath. 'Oh Jubilee!'

I have said elsewhere that we do not choose symbols, they choose us. And I did not choose Mr Blagger, for instance, nor his attributes. I had no idea when he first appeared why he was always in a basement room playing patience, why his clock ticked so loudly, why he sat so still and rooted. But I think I know now. I think I have solved the riddle.

The kinds of meanings I have been talking about are really a substructure, underpinnings to what is on the surface a story. But I believe it is these underlying meanings that give the story power, even if not the faintest hint of them is consciously apparent to the reader. Much of the strength of a book, much of its real essence, is subliminal. The words are merely the tip of an iceberg. And if I anticipate another question, 'Do children really understand all this, does any of it come through to them?' my answer is an unequivocal 'Yes'.

I have a strong feeling now, as an adult, that I am practically a result of what I read as a child, and yet I am sure that I did not 'understand', in the sense of being able to formulate as an idea, even a fraction of what I read. But in reading, as in life, ninety per cent of what we experience, we experience as it were through the pores, and it comes to us directly without our translating it at all. We do not go through life constantly saying to ourselves 'I am now looking at the grass' or 'I can now feel a draught blowing on my neck', but these kinds of things are happening the whole time and are present to us in some way. The whole time things are filtering through direct, as it were, by-passing our conscious awareness. Paradoxically, then, one almost reads the real substance between the lines of a book.

I have said that I write partly in order to find out, and in a sense I do not know what I mean until I have said it. And in the same way as I am operating on this level as a writer, so the reader too is experiencing things which he recognizes but has no words for. This is partly what any kind of reading does. It makes accessible all kinds of floating feelings and attitudes and ideas which probably have never been crystallized before.

Now I have said some things to explain what I think certain of my books are about – it is, after all, my privilege, since I wrote them. But at the same time I think there is a very real danger in people taking books apart in this way. They should rest content with experiencing the book. That is all that is required in the way of response. I do not work out my books consciously, and so for someone to go about analysing them consciously is an irrelevant if not actually damaging process. And of course any book can be all things to all men, or put another way, certain things to certain people. A book is in a sense a mirror. I quote Lichtenberg again: 'A book is a mirror: if an ass peers into it, you can't expect an apostle to look out.'

I have had a man come up to me after a meeting and ask me, in all seriousness, whether or not I realized that the pie dish in *The Piemakers* is a symbol of the Ark of the Covenant. Now I think I can state with perfect truth that I had not realized this, nor do I, even after much hard and conscientious thought, realize it now. (I am not even entirely sure that I know what the Ark of the Covenant is.) The gentleman in question of course has every right to his theory (though it is not incumbent on a reader to have any theory at all) but if he does have one, all that is necessary is for him to keep it to himself.

A book is in a sense a private dialogue between one writer and one reader, and as subjective an experience as any other in life. And for one reader, however clever, to go round propagating the theory that a perfectly (well, almost) straightforward pie dish is anything other than just that, is merely to confuse, irritate, and even damage. Let it not be forgotten that we can read into anything almost anything we want. I once went through what I consider one of the tamest of my books, *The Signposters*, as an exercise, looking for phallic symbols, and had a very nasty shock, indeed. The thing is a veritable Freudian field day. There are church spires, ladders, sun's rays and candles bristling on practically every page, not to mention valleys, umbrellas and, I ask you, tents.

I gave this piece its title because I think much of what I write is ancient, in the sense that there is nothing new under the sun, but modern in that it embodies the attitudes not of the present establishment of technology, reason and materialism, but of the underground resistance to it. If the Bongleweed were a political party, I would vote for it. And this is where we come to the 'incorrigibly plural': 'The Bongleweed was a sign that all things are possible.'

If there is one phrase that has recurred over and over again in my work and thinking right from adolescence, when I first used it, that phrase is 'infinite possibility'. And I think I was trying to personify this in *The Bongleweed* by making the weed the hero of the book. I have been reliably informed by an unimpeachable psychological authority that the Bongle-weed is a symbol of the creative imagination, and am happy to say that by the time I was told this I had already worked it out for myself.

The children in the story, and the Finches, who are themselves intuitive and childlike, love the Bongleweed at sight:

> She stared up at it and saw how deliciously new and green it was and the sun was lathering it with gold and the magic of the thing was plain to see, indisputable. It grew under the moon and under the sun, it put out branches and threw out leaves with an extravagance that looked to Becky like sheer joy at being alive. And it was going to ramp all over the graveyard, she could see that, so it certainly had no respect for the dead. In short, it was a friend.

But to the establishment, to Dr Harper with his scientific hubris, with his insistence on facts, with his strong urge to categorize – 'It was all so *unbotanical!*' – the Bongleweed is a threat, with its 'careless lack of consideration for walls, boundaries, rules – even for the laws of nature'. The reaction of the typical adult is either to ignore it in the hope that it will go away, or failing that to chop – destroy. The experts do not like to be confronted by the inexplicable (an expert, as I define him, being a man who holds the subjective belief that we must all be objective). But children do, because they have not yet been fixed into conventional stances, because they have not yet been forced to make false boundaries and divisions, because they are still aware that life *is* 'incorrigibly plural' and glory in the knowledge, instead of forcing it away as an unpalatable truth.

The Bongleweed comes into the world as a figment of Becky's imagination, but is able to convert only the already converted. When the ordinary people come out of church and pause to look at the incomparable beauty of the weed that has transformed the graveyard:

. . . it seemed to Becky even from that distance that they were nowhere near astonished enough. They could not have even half realized how strange a thing had happened in their midst, or even half seen how beautiful it was. They paused, looked, and in the end turned and walked on.

. . . And she hated them all, for the Bongleweed's sake. It had done everything it could, thrown out its prodigal gifts of flower and greenery, burned itself out, for all she knew, to make things new again, to show them a first morning. But no one was looking.

'Except us', she thought.

And for the Bongleweed that, surely, was cold comfort.

Cold comfort indeed. I wish it could have been otherwise but sometimes the truth, despite oneself, must contain pessimism. But no absolute pessimism. The Bongleweed is not merely something in its own right, but also a *sign* of something. And so when it dies, as it naturally must, Becky knows that this is not really the end, nor anything like it:

In a world where once a Bongleweed has sprung, anything would be possible, from now on. Perhaps *another* Bongleweed, clinging tenaciously to life down among the frosted roots, ready to wax again in the warmth and showers of April. Or perhaps it would be something quite different – out of the blue – desperate, beautiful, reckless – *anything*!

She opened her eyes and glared fiercely down at the innocent, melting garden where the white was almost visibly yielding now to the green.

'You wait!' she thought exultantly. 'Just you wait!'

Becky opened the window and felt her skin shrivel. She leaned right out above the blackened branches of the Bongleweed and drew in the heady smell of frost and was at once certain, in her very bones, that the world itself was both alert and mysterious as those foxes' heads had been. The world had gone once and forever wild on her very doorstep.

And here I rest my case.

# 16

# ONE THUMPING LIE ONLY
## *Nicholas Fisk*

*The Princess of the School, The Chums of the Remove, Pip, Squeak and Wilfred, Fiona and her Ponies, Eric or Little by Little* – where are you now? The answer is, mouldering on my bookshelves. *My* bookshelves, not those of my children and their friends. To them, Dimsie, Head Girl, is rather more unlikely than a Moon Man. Yesterday's children got what was good for them. Today's children get what they want. One of the things they don't want very much is a book. Literacy itself is becoming yet another commodity in short supply.

Which poses a problem for the children's writer. However much he loves his craft – the act of devising and writing stories – he must still send his product to market. A typescript is merely a pupa. There can be no real life for the creature until it has been released by the publisher. So the writer must consider his market. What is the children's-book market? It is almost entirely an adult business. Adults commission, condition, review and distribute the writer's work. The buyer is not very often a child. Children buy, or get someone else to buy for them, a particular toy: not many children buy books.

Yet the child recipient of a book makes judgements that may be crucial. Certain children's writers succeed in the face of opposition from librarians and educationists. Other writers, producing work that deserves and gets high praise from adults, find that their work brings nothing more tangible than rose-coloured exhalations of esteem.

What is the writer to do? Should he stubbornly and devotedly aim to satisfy only himself, or should he conduct a market survey and set himself to conform with its findings? Should he consult his peers – the adults who establish the children's-book market – or should he talk to the children themselves and hope to learn something from them?

Whichever course he follows (and most probably he will try all of them at one time or another) he will find no certain answers. A book is not a Go/No-Go product. It cannot be balanced like columns of figures, or checked with ruler and setsquare, or made to resume ticking if it stops. So even if the writer is certain of the excellence of his work on Monday, he may think very differently on Tuesday. Again, if his market survey reveals a definite trend and demand, it may be that the publishers are seeking an innovation. Yet again, even the most expert and sympathetic of his peers have bees in their bonnets that buzz a note different from the writer's.

This leaves the children themselves. They make unreliable and disturbing guides.

Unreliable, because the tastes of the majority are bounded by what they already know. New ideas and possibilities are not necessarily attractive to them (the proof of the pudding is puddings: try adding sherry to the nursery trifle. Or if the nursery trifle has always had sherry in it, try serving it without). Disturbing, because the more children one meets, the more clearly the dedicated writer realizes how minutely small his audience is. Forty-nine children in fifty will ask the visiting writer if he has ever been on telly? – how long does it take to write a book? – do you get a lot of money? Only one child in fifty asks the questions that matter; for example, 'Do you have trouble finding titles?', or 'Have you ever found a title so good that you couldn't make the story fit it?' (This writer was asked the last question by a small coloured boy wearing large spectacles. Professional spoke to professional in that moment.)

Despite the gap between oneself, the writer, and forty-nine out of fifty children (much the same ratio, after all, holds good in adult relationships), there are still conclusions the writer must reach and hold to, right or wrong, if he is to produce anything at all. My conclusions are as follows.

Book-reading children have changed. Once, the majority of child readers – the middle-class owners of Rackham's latest, say – were a separate tribe who, ideally, spoke when they were spoken to and did as they were bid. Today, the nurseryless child lives in the company of adults, occupying the same rooms, joining in the family conversations and (most important) watching many of the same TV programmes. No Christopher Robin, this child. He has a smattering of adult phrases and attitudes. He appears harder, tougher, more of the world. His teddy bear, if he has one, wears a space helmet. His sister's wardrobe is supplied by fashion houses. Both are, quite consciously, 'consumers'.

A veneer? Not all of it. Just as your grownup son seems to have instinctive mastery over car engines and your eighteen-year-old daughter seems to acquire an immediate and esteemed place in commerce, so today's children have a flair for the world they live in – a world in whose spindle Communication, Acquisition and Technology are embedded like 'Brighton' in pink rock. The children are better informed than ever they were about what makes things tick, how many beans make five, the Wankel engine, the pre-teen brassiere and a host of concepts and articles that never entered the minds of the Rackham child. (Conversely, this same child may adopt Rackham in the late teens and early twenties.)

This is not to say that the 'tender' attributes of childhood are lost. Children still on occasion trail clouds of glory. Their eyes remain large and wondering. Their minds still have room for fantasy and fanaticism, myth and romance. It is just that their range, experience and admiration for the tangible have increased disproportionately.

What can one write for these children? Even if everything said in the preceding paragraph is untrue, it still provides a table capable of supporting a typewriter. Children are more technological, more hardware-conscious? Then write about twentieth-century things. Children are more experienced in techniques of communication? Then write faster narratives and pay less attention to old devices thought necessary to link and clarify a story. Children are less literate than they were – less able to understand the long words used by the author, of, say, the William books? Then ignore their ignorance and insist that they keep pace with you, the writer. Adults, too, must be permitted to express themselves.

This said and the typewriter firmly supported, it still remains necessary to fill the page. With what? For myself, the dilemma has solved itself by a process of elimination. I began, nervously, by writing childish little books for little children; my only security was provided by precedent and a well-stocked bookshelf. Watching my own children and their friends (and reading what I had written) obliged me to mend my ways. My child readers might, occasionally, be persuaded to share my nostalgias and fancies – even my childhood – but this was not to be relied on. Better to devise stories that belonged either to a period the reader would recognize – the period of *now*; or to go so far back, or so far forward, that the reader must simply take my word for it.

*Now* had little to offer. As an adult, I cannot share my reader's experiences, nor have I the Dickensian skills needed to transmogrify the present – to make something large as life and twice as natural. And in any case, for myself alone, the present means nothing very much. Like the Deal faith-healer, on the whole I dislike what I fancy I feel. How much better to board an era liner and travel into new times, possibilities and situations! How much more exciting the microscope's or telescope's viewpoint than one's own! How much more interesting the possibility than the fact; the drawn conclusion than the stated premise; the freedom of fantasy than the chains of present circumstance!

I began to write what is misnamed science fiction – stories centred on concepts, possibilities, extension and fantasy. The subject matter suggests itself; indeed, tattered, disjointed applicants for a role knock on the door of my brain at night, insisting on auditions. 'I am a nice old lady,' says one of these apparitions, 'but not old at all. And not a lady. And certainly not nice . . . Can't you do something for me?' 'I am a cloud of shiny, glittering particles,' says another, 'raining from a clear sky. I am here for a purpose. Could you oblige me by telling me what purpose?'

These two applicants were exorcized by completing books about them. Others crowd in to take their place. Many are attractive. They make great promises. Living up to their promises, however, invariably turns out to be the responsibility of the author. The Muse has never delivered for me the package complete.

Nor has my own hard, untidy, infuriating work of plotting a story ever yet resulted in a wholly rounded, wholly satisfactory, Creation. The story of the nice old lady who is no such thing, for example, is necessarily incomplete. The book resolves her essential mystery, but her inessentials remain tantalizing, at least to her creator. Do beings from other worlds have pets? Do their children bite whatever is the equivalent of their fingernails? Do relations visit them at inconvenient times?

The questions sound frivolous, but are not. The basis of successful fantasy in believable realism. The White Rabbit in *Alice* comes alive when he takes out his pocket watch and cries, 'I'm late.'

Another rule I have made for myself is to eschew any story that is resolved by saying, for example, 'When she awoke she rubbed her eyes and said, "Why, it was only a dream after all!"' Carroll is allowed this sort of thing, but not the present-day writer addressing a hard-headed audience, nearing its teens. The plot can be allowed one thumping lie (say, the invasion of Earth), but only one. Everything arising from the thumping lie must make sense.

It must also involve children, which, on first thoughts, seems difficult. But really it is not. In *Grinny* – the story about the nice old lady who was nothing of the sort – the children were the undeniably logical exception to the general rule that People Are Powerless. Only children would serve the writer's purpose, which was to supply, for the invaders, a control by which to measure the success of their experiment.

So the characteristics of children can be peculiarly apt to the needs of the writer of fantastic but realistic stories. Children are alert, adaptable, fully equipped miniatures of adults, lacking only such important qualities as experience and authority. The practical effects of these deficiencies have been exploited in countless stories (*The Go-Between* is one of them) and, for the children's writer, the attributes and limitations of children are a boon rather than a bane.

All the more so if the writer is attempting fantasy. The reactions of his child characters to fantastic events and situations is more limited, direct, unequivocal and economical; and therefore more malleable, in the 'potter's clay' sense. One can do things to or with child characters that would be inadmissible or illogical if adults were the protagonists.

There are corresponding disadvantages. Though children's books are adult concoctions, one must still play fair by the child readers. It would be unfair, for example, to write a children's novel centred on the adventures of a child who finds himself in an apparently endless corridor arranged as a Moebius strip – yet a first-rate 'science fiction' story was written, for adults, on this premise. You yourself may not know what a Moebius strip is, but you can easily find out. A child cannot.

Then there is the question, touched on earlier, of syntax. The author of the *William* books quite simply ignored the problem and wrote as she pleased; the books were and are a raging success with children, who allow themselves to be towed over the bumpy bits by the impetus of the narrative. As words themselves – even if only half understood – create atmosphere, sensation, magic and so on, this approach seems right: the writer says what he wants to say – re-reads it – then prunes or adds words in the hope of finding the right combination of sense and sensibility. A slim hope, perhaps, but worth clinging to: most written words, never mind whether their readers are adults or children are only partly understood. A letter about a machine that does not work, or an involved family matter, seldom produces a relevant response. The manufacturer replies by talking about the terms of his guarantee; the family letter produces a completely separate crisis from Aunt Rose, who knew all along that nobody really liked her.

At least the fiction writer has the reader on his side. The reader *wants* to understand his words and translate them into appropriate thoughts and emotions. One reward for the children's writer comes from the occasional evidence of this understanding – a letter in big wobbly writing, signed 'your friend, Susan (age 7)'. She was too young fully to have understood the writer's meanings but she understood enough.

There are other rewards. It is arguable that the highest expression of humankind takes the form of a child. It is very easy indeed to argue that the human mind is at its most agile, adventurous, generous and receptive stage during childhood. So the children's writer is mixing with and working for the Right People.

It is even possible to persuade oneself that by writing for children, one is doing some good. All the clichés about rat races and consumer societies are true, just as it is always true that the country is going to the dogs. It is a wonderful thing to crash the grey barriers – and all the more worthwhile if you can take the children with you.

# 17

# ON NOT WRITING
# A PROPER BOOK

## *K. M. Peyton*

I HAVE no strongly held theories on 'writing for children'. An honest writer writes first and finds the appropriate market, if it exists. His bad luck if it doesn't. I don't myself even subscribe to the idea that one sets out to be a writer; one writes, and if the work sells and eventually enables one to make a living from it, one presumably is a writer. If the writing is sold to children, one is a children's writer. I set out to be a painter, and became a teacher, which I liked very much; but I was a writer all the time, and eventually this became my profession.

Why one becomes a children's writer rather than a writer for adults is another matter. I became a children's writer because I started writing as a child and naturally wrote children's books. Since then I must have suffered some sort of mental retardment, for I still write, as I did then, the sort of stories I like writing best and my audience is still young, whereas I am now gone forty. My mother asks me, 'When are you going to write a proper book?' 'They *are* proper books,' I reply stiffly. I have thought seriously about starting on a novel about adults, but there is nothing in me that wants to do it. I go in the car and meet the girls off the train from school, or, occasionally, my husband from London. It is, perhaps, seven o'clockish, going dark, raining, and the train is late. Around me are several other cars with lone women in them, also waiting for their husbands. Some of them have already moved into the passenger seat (which I consider an odd thing to do, and so fortunately does my husband). This is when I most often think about writing an adult novel. If I ever do, it will start with a woman in a car meeting her husband off the train. She will have two teenage girls who are being difficult, and her husband is having an affair with another woman. I get as far as this and dry up. My mind always goes to the teen-age girls being difficult – full of rich possibilities. The housewife's problem doesn't worry me. If I try and pursue it, the story becomes wooden in my head. The adult situation bores me.

Characters in my mind die on me after the age of twenty. I follow them thus far, enjoying them enormously, but after that I lose interest. I don't ever even want to know what happens to them after I have finished with them. There is possibly some psychological reason for this that a trained person might be able to explain to me; I hope I haven't inadvertently revealed some highly embarrassing truth about myself of which I am still ignorant.

Books reveal all. It is the occupational hazard one learns to accept, only hoping that the reader is too interested in the story to wonder about what prompted it to be written. When I was small my books were locked away and no one was ever allowed to read them, except the one favoured publisher's editor on whom I conferred the honour. When he had returned it I locked it away again. But when I eventually got published, the agony of realizing that anyone could read what I had written was considerable, and for years I wrote with a certain caution, not always putting down exactly what I would have liked for fear of appearing a bit soppy· Later, with more confidence, I wrote it all down and got labelled a 'romantic' writer. This is a highly dangerous label which I am scrupulously conscious of. And yet, should anyone tax me to defend myself, I could quote such actual, factual incidents that have happened to me that my critic would (I hope) be quite confounded. I wrote an article once for the *Guardian* (which at that time accepted most of what I sent them) about what had happened to me on my first 'exchange' visit to France at the age of sixteen, and Mrs Stott sent it back saying how much she had enjoyed it, but of course could not publish it as it obviously wasn't true. Every word of it was true, in fact, but I didn't stoop to defend myself. Later, while I was writing *The Maplin Bird*, what was happening to me in my sailing life was more shattering than anything endured by Emily on board her smack; writing of her sufferings came very easily after my own shipwreck and rescue, and the true story of the life-saving suit invented by the hero's brother in *The Plan for Birdsmarsh* was far more eventful in fact than I made it in fiction. Much of this 'eventfulness' in my life can be laid to my husband's account, his mottoes being 'Do it now' and – afterwards – 'All for the best.'

One's books can only be built on one's own experiences. Which ones, at the time, one cannot always foresee. A quiet and lovely autumn afternoon searching for the grave of the Pytchley hounds drowned through the ice in 1910 in the grounds of the now derelict Fawsley Manor, eventually turned into a book, although at the time it wasn't at all what I was doing it for. I was doing it because it was what I wanted to do – and perhaps, if one wants to be analytical, it was a childlike thing to do, for it entailed struggling through a mass of brambles and going down on hands and knees under ancient laurel bushes in a wilderness of what had once been a garden, not exactly what the other visitors were doing, whose cars were parked alongside mine in the car park. I did not foresee that regularly eavesdropping on the conversation of some schoolboys on a train when I came home once a week with the shopping would grow into *Pennington's Seventeenth Summer* (with the real-life Pennington spectacularly saving a man from drowning in the river during a Force 8 gale and being presented with a real-life medal). Nor did I realize that a dabbling in music which started with the children's recorder lessons in the village school would lead me to the complexities of following Pennington in his virtuoso career – and I shall be eternally grateful to that particular hero for driving me to learn to play the piano, which ironically has made more inroads into my 'writing-time' than any of my other commitments.

When I get frustrated by the demands of these other commitments deflecting me from the writing, I console myself that they are the lifeblood of what I am writing about, and that the ivory tower, attractive as it may appear at times, would not suit. The male writer, quiet in his room with coffee and lunch served, the interruptions deflected by a devoted wife, is at times my great envy; but at other times I feel that the very frustrations are somehow a part of my driving force. My most difficult book to date, *A Pattern of Roses*, was written through the winter when a forty-foot boat was being built full-time in the garden and a constant stream of nautical maniacs was in and out of the house at all times, drinking coffee and needing hungry labourer's meals, as many as twenty-four one weekend. I have no help at home, and consider myself fairly fully occupied with the normal ferrying of schoolchildren, housework and looking after five horses (since, in desperation, cut down to two) – the horses, like the piano, are time-consumers, but necessary. It was during this winter that one of the horses, lent by a farmer from the village three miles away, used to get out of the field and go home, sometimes taking the other four with her, at a flat gallop. When this happened in the middle of the night my husband used to turn over in bed and remind me, as we listened to the departing clatter of hooves down the lane, that the horses were my department; his was the boat. But out of these calamities, nice cameos remain: creeping through someone's back garden with headcollar in hand, dressed in long nightdress, anorak and gum-boots, and being speared by torchlight from the bedroom window, or returning home in the car with my daughter riding the mare ahead in the light from the headlamps, cantering fast along the verge with only a halter for tack, and me thinking, 'Oh, God, if she falls off the mare will go all the way back again . . .'

I think now that if I only had a book to write, and nothing else to do, I would just sit and stare into space. To know that on Tuesday, for in- stance, Fred will call for coffee and chat at half-past ten, the butcher will interrupt at eleven fifteen and want to know what I shall want next Friday, and that I've got to get to the nearest shop, three miles away, to buy a loaf before it shuts at one, concentrates the mind wonderfully. My mother needs to talk to me at length twice a week at least, a pony needs shoeing (five miles there and five miles back and an hour in the middle), and in the summer the garden and the field are a full-time job (mine). It is no good at all pleading my vocation, for my only local claim to fame is not in writing but as Secretary of the Pony Club, and when this keeps me almost fully occupied throughout the summer months I console myself by the richness of the material I am building up in this direction. The fact that pony books are now out of fashion, a relic of the nineteen thirties and forties, will not deter me from embarking on this saga before long, so eagerly does the spring bubble up. Where would I be without my inter- ruptions? Still staring at a blank sheet in the typewriter.

The fact is, I like writing very much, better than anything else. I write to entertain, but whether I'm entertaining them or myself I've never quite decided. Sometimes I think it is more for them, sometimes for me. This is not to say that I don't find writing hard work; the concentration required in the actual doing is considerable, and the hours of just thinking about it are very long, if perfectly pleasant. I do most of this in bed, on trains and on long sailing holidays, and when gardening, peeling potatoes, cleaning the windows, washing the kitchen floor, etc. Not when driving the car, which I've proved is dangerous. What it is all for, entertainment apart, I could not say. Does it have to be justified? Whether it cleanses one of one's hang-ups, a personal therapy disguised as art, or whether one is trying to wield an influence in the wide world, I could not say. I certainly do not feel it this way, but these motives are put. When a writer knows he has a juvenile audience, a certain responsibility is inevitably felt, but to think that he can 'con' his audience into what might be called correct attitudes must be doomed to failure. The writer's own attitudes probably show through, but whether these are uplifting or depressing depends on who is the judge. I feel that the only possible limitation in writing in this sphere is the necessity to write within the framework of the reader's understanding, but as this is as wide or as narrow as the writer cares to make it (as wide, for example, as set by Alan Garner in *The Owl Service* or as narrow as the view of Enid Blyton in the Famous Five or Secret Seven series), it is scarcely to be thought of as limiting. I have not yet found this a difficulty, and when I do I suppose the time will have come to write 'a proper book'. Until then I shall continue as I am.

# 18

# THE LAST LORD OF
# REDHOUSE CASTLE

*Mollie Hunter*

'THE last lord of Redhouse Castle,' said Mr Miller, 'was hanged for murdering his brother.'

My spine tingled – or, as we in Scotland would say – 'a grue ran up my back'; not unnaturally, of course, since I was only twelve years old at this time. Mr Miller being elderly, and also the learned President of our village Literary Society, had a more sophisticated outlook on fratricide.

' – belonged to the family of the Black Douglases,' I caught his voice smoothly continuing, 'and there was a secret tunnel to the sea, down which it was said the murderer tried to make his escape.'

*Hush thee, hush thee, dinna fret ye; the Black Douglas willna get ye.*

Ever since I could remember, it seemed to me, I had known that sinister little lullaby. But was the Black Douglas of Redhouse Castle also the one in the song? The one who had risen from the shadows on the curtain walk of another castle, and laying a mailed hand on the shoulder of a woman singing her child to sleep with that same lullaby, had said quietly, grimly:

*'I wouldna be too sure o' that!'*

I would find out, I promised myself. I would study history properly and find out lots of things. Which indeed I did; and also about Celtic folk-lore, which became my other love. Yet strangely, for all the faithful years in love's service, it was only belatedly in my attempts to make a career as a writer that I thought of using all the material I had researched. As for the shape that career would take, it was even longer before I realized it would be that of a children's writer.

Mind you, I like children. I like their interest and enthusiasm. Their comparative lack of inhibition sorts well with my own ebullience, and in their company I am easy. Furthermore, I was born with the gift of the gab and the instinct to perform, and there is no better spotlight than the attention of children.

All of which adds up to the fact that I have always enjoyed telling stories to children – my own included. Occasionally also, I enjoyed taking time off from other forms of writing to set down some of these stories. Nevertheless, it was still only at the insistence of my two young sons that I wrote my first children's book, they being much charmed with two short stories I had written for them in a style which was then new to me.

There was an old, old device, however, at the heart of this style; the device on which I have since hung all the books my publishers call fantasies, and which I have borrowed from Celtic folk-lore.

A voice is implied, and as in folk-lore, the voice sounds as if recounting a familiar and accepted tale in which fact is seamlessly integrated with fancy. The modern story-teller, however, does not have an audience conditioned to accept and believe in all those incidents of the supernatural which give folk-lore its dramatic dimensions, and thus a further device is required to make such fantasies credible.

Quickly, on to the matter-of-fact opening scene, there must be brought characters with an equally matter-of-fact acknowledgment of certain superstitious beliefs and customs – and it makes no difference whether this acknowledgment is a scornful or a believing one. The seed has been sown. The reader has felt the touch of the Otherworld on his shoulder; and imperceptibly from this point, so imperceptibly that no-one notices the actual moment of lift-off, the story can soar into fantasy.

The stories I had already attempted on these lines concerned a foolish boastful Irishman called Patrick Kentigern Keenan. I liked Patrick. My sons persisted in wanting 'a proper book about Patrick', but my foolish hero by this time had discovered for me the pitfalls in trying to reproduce the authentic voice of folk-lore.

*I will take the world for my pillow.* Thus the hero of the Celtic tale speaks, traditionally, as he sets out on a journey which is also a quest through life. Thus the narrative of folk-lore flows in a style as spare and smooth as polished bone; and thus the high poetic insight of its verbal imagery. And so I hesitated. Yet the challenge of such an exercise in language excited me. There were all sorts of folk-lore beliefs I wanted to work into such a book, and the turns of speech so characteristic of the Celt were mine by right of birth and upbringing. Besides which, the spotlight was on me. . . !

I had given my Patrick the gift of laughter, a wife patiently enduring of his folly, and a young son dearly loved. Now I set him growing in stature as he pursued a running conflict in which he lost every battle, yet always learned a little wisdom in the process. And gained a small loser's prize too, for Patrick's opponents were fairies who always left some trace of their magic behind them – but no gossamer-winged sprites of the modern picture-book, these fairies!

These were the lordly and beautiful ones of the hollow hills; the skilful magicians of the Otherworld, the soul-less ones who were the ancient terror of men . . . I sensed the grue running up my children's backs as I read, the fascination of being within touching distance of that terror – yet always with the comfort of knowing there was Patrick's saving grace of laughter between it and them, always aware of the safe ground of human warmth to which they could retreat.

Until the moment finally came when it seemed there was no more room for laughter, or courage, or cunning; for this was the moment when Patrick's small son became a hostage in the conflict with the fairies, and Patrick was stripped of every weapon save his great love for the boy.

Yet still the hostage did not become the victim, for this – the love of one human for another – is the very thing the soul-less ones can never experience or understand, and over which they have therefore no power. And so Patrick won home with his son, not permanently sobered by his experience, but almost a wise man at last. So at last, also, the children had their 'proper book' about him, and in basing its outcome on the triumph of human love over the dark powers of the soul-less ones, I had laid the cornerstone of my whole life's philosophy.

Before I realized this latter was the case, however, I had a lot more writing to do, alternating further fantasies with historical novels for children; for now I had discovered the great seed-bed of fertility all those years of research had laid down in my mind. Ideas were sprouting fast. The story-telling current was running strong, carrying with it an uneasy feeling lingering from my own childhood days.

That scarecrow in the field, ragged, its faceless head drooping – what if it should suddenly lift its head? The faceless one show suddenly it had a face? *What kind of face would I see?*

The grue again! That sense of something from the past touching me! A figure loomed up out of my researches into Scottish history – James the Fifth, 'the poor man's king'. King Jamie at his favourite ploy of roaming his kingdom in disguise – he would be my scarecrow! Almost before I realized what had happened I was writing *Hi, Johnny*, my first historical novel; and inevitably, because my own children were so interested in it, it was a book for children.

And so it was with my second of the same; for, as it was pointed out to me, it would be so much easier for the publisher to decide on acceptance of the first if they knew I had one to follow. I heard the spotlight clicking on, and with the cue-line, *But I have!* sprang into my act.

I was back in my favourite sixteenth century, in Edinburgh, my favourite of cities. I knew the time as well as I know my own; the plan of the city as intimately as the lay-out of my own garden. I could feel the cobbles of the High Street slippery under my feet, smell the ordure piled in the closes and vennels opening off it, see the lights of Holyrood Palace, and hear the State secrets whispered there reaching me as clearly as did the gossip of the change-house at its gates. Above all, I knew the character of my sixteenth-century Edinburgh, and this was the character of the boy who emerged from the story I told impromptu that day – Jamie Morton, hero of *The Spanish Letters*; a fifteen-year-old as tough, proud, dirty, and honest as the city which had bred him.

Jamie, the sixteenth-century street-boy, was also my challenge to the cosy tradition of middle-class heroes in historical novels for children; and with satisfaction, when I came to write this book, I knew I was not addressing it to the privileged minority of readers for whom the tradition had been invented. I was writing it for all those in the shared state of being called childhood; and charging headlong with Jamie, I was going to demolish the barriers which prevented that sharing.

There were problems in all this, of course; the first being the one peculiar to Scottish writers in this field – how to set the scene in a country whose history is unknown to non-Scottish children. Secondly, I had to deal with an extension of the difficulty facing all writers attempting to convey the flavour of period dialogue without falling into the 'prithee' and 'sirrah' bog; for any dialogue in a Lowland Scots setting had also to give at least the impression of being conducted in the dialect proper to it. In narrative also, the Scot naturally uses dialect words which are infinitely richer in meaning than their nearest equivalent in standard English, and since I was determined to retain this native piquancy of expression, I had to find ways of making it self-explanatory in context.

The first 'historical' had been my 'prentice effort to cope with these problems. The second was my journeyman piece, and I emerged from it professional enough to know that this had been satisfactorily completed.

One other thing I knew was that a book altogether different from these two was growing in my mind, and that I had to write it.

Its scene was the Scottish Highlands. The time was the nineteenth century when thousands of poor crofting folk were 'cleared' – a euphemism for being driven with guns and dogs and whips from their native glens – to make way for sheep-farming. The incident which had gripped my imagination was that of a boy in the glen called Greenyards, unexpectedly pulling a pistol on a Sheriff Officer serving writs of evacuation there; and through this action, appearing briefly in history as the central figure in a short, doomed resistance to that particular clearance.

This boy haunted me. Looking at Ardgay Hill, from whence he and the other children of the glen had kept watch for the arrival of the Sheriff's forces, I found the thought of those other children also haunting me. I read letters, diaries, newspapers of the period. I talked to old people with intimate experience of crofting life, and got from them old tales and childhood memories. In Gaelic-speaking company I sat apart, letting the music of the old tongue fill my ears. Summer day after summer day I left my own comfortable home in the Highlands to wander among the poor little ruins of stone houses which mark the sites of the clearances, and the pain of the parting which had happened there was keen again.

I knew much already of the Highlander's passionate, almost mystic attachment to his native land. Now I was reliving the despair of spirit which had filled them in the knowledge they were being driven from it, never to return. I was touching the edge of a sorrow so great that some of these people had literally died of it. But how to convey all this in a story for children? How to convey also the sense of kinship among these people, their respect for learning, their innate courtesy? Most of all, how to convey the courage of that pathetic little resistance?

I needed a new writing technique for this. I had my journeyman skill as a novelist. In the three fantasies I had written by this time, I had continued to refine the art of projecting verbal imagery. Now I needed to synthesize these separate skills into a first-person narrative spoken swiftly, bitterly, angrily, yet still with all the beauty of phrasing which comes naturally to the Highland tongue. And because children were an integral part of my story, it was the voice of a boy that was called for – the boy who had pulled the pistol on the Sheriff Officer in Greenyards.

I was unaware at the time of thinking this out, of course, that I was one with other iconoclasts then busily breaking all the rules previously observed in writing for children. I live in isolation from other writers, and always have done. To my publishers' cry that nobody, but *nobody* had heard of the Highland Clearances, I turned a deaf ear. I brushed aside their objections to the bloody – but true – incident in which a posse of constables batoned a group of unresisting women and children almost to death.

Nor did it even occur to me that I was ripping away convention in allowing the voice of poetry to come through a boy's narrative; or by drawing this boy's character in depth so that, by showing all the linking strands of his emotions, I could also show the emotions of his people.

I had figured out a method of presenting the brutality of the attack on the women in a manner which would cause the young reader to rise in indignation rather than recoil in horror. I was eager to meet the challenge of language in my chosen medium. I had my title – *A Pistol in Greenyards*. And clearest of all in my mind was a picture of the children who had kept watch on Ardgay Hill.

I felt a rage of pity for the innocent courage of these children. For they were real – they had lived through what I had to tell. And surely one child could cry out to another over any gap of years? Surely, surely, it was possible for other children to hear the courage in the cry? With a sense of total involvement in the lives of my characters, I wrote the first sentence of their story, setting its beginning on the emigrant ship carrying them away, in defeat, from the beloved glen: '*I saw him coming along the deck of the ship towards me, and even though I owed him my life, I hated the very look of him.*'

The book which grew from this was dedicated to the children who had kept watch on Ardgay Hill, and to their descendants; and by an odd chance, not long after it was published, I happened to meet one of these descendants – a grandson of one of the watchers. Many and many a time, this man told me, he had heard his grandfather telling of how it was in the clearance of Greenyards. And, he added, when he read my book:

'It could have been my grandfather himself talking.'

I had already noted the compulsive force this book had exerted on the elder of my sons, although he was not by that time particularly interested in historical novels. Now the writer in me preened at this tribute – the one of all others which told me I had succeeded in what I had set out to do – and something dark which had been couching at the door of my mind began to diminish in size. But not to vanish entirely. That was not to happen until several books later, when I was walking alone in the hills around my home and thinking deeply of the fantasy then engaging me.

As always, on these occasions, I was keenly aware of the delight of manipulating language at its two extremes of exactitude and subtlety. The quiet of the glen held a sound beyond silence. The light on the hills had the gentle, ever-changing quality unique to the Highlands, necessary for the vision beyond sight; and as always, listening and watching like this, I became aware of my mind operating on two levels.

A blacksmith goes poaching. He finds evidence of a hare caught in one of his traps, but the trap has been destroyed by something infinitely more powerful than a hare. A boy makes a whistle. He plays on it some music remembered from a dream, and finds he has discovered the secret of a call belonging to a dangerous and unnatural enemy. A young farmer ploughs land that has always before been left fallow, and finds that his action has also disturbed a dark and deadly magic.

This was the superficial level on which I had created *The Haunted Mountain*, and other fantasies; the level of the suspense story in which ordinary people suddenly encounter creatures from the Otherworld, and which a young reader could relish simply for the drama of events unfolded by the encounter. On the deeper level, however, I was continuing to pursue the philosophy which had led me to climax the first fantasy with the triumph of human love over the dark power of the soul-less ones; and it was language used like a sharp tool which enabled me to penetrate to this depth, for here the suspense came from that duality of feeling which traditionally characterizes men's attitude to the Otherworld itself.

It was a world of perfection which held for them all the attraction of a golden age; a world without sickness, pain, or death, yet still a world without love in it, and thus hollow at the heart. For this was the world of the beautiful soul-less ones; and any man who entered it would be hopelessly in their thrall and became prisoner – as they were – of their desolate Eden.

And so, always between themselves and the temptation to enter this world, men interposed the barrier of this fearful knowledge. Always, for those who had been abducted to it, they clung to the redeeming promise in the power of human love. For this, men have always dimly known, is the essential of their lives. This is the thread in folk-lore that binds Greece to Connemara. That a man should retain the power to look up and see the face of his God – whatever face that god may wear. That a man should be able to stretch out a hand in the illimitable darkness of eternity, and always from somewhere in that darkness, feel the warmth and comforting touch of another human hand.

A one-to-one contact between man and God, and between man and man; this is all that ultimately matters.

This, too, is something known instinctively to the child young enough to be responding still to the pull of the wholly fantasy world of his very early years, yet still reluctant to lose the foothold he has just gained on the real world. In the half-remembered fantasy world, there are terrors lurking; in the real world, a certainty of safety. Thus, it seems to me, even the child reading the story at its superficial level will be touched by something of its underlying philosophy. As he feels the touch of the Otherworld in the prickle of his skin, so will he feel the emanation of this philosophy in a prickling of his mind. And even although the mind-prickling will be incomprehensible to him at the time, some day he may associate it with his own philosophic strivings; and remembering, will understand.

These were conclusions which, as I walked that day, I knew I had long ago formed. I knew also that I was enormously fortunate to have found a medium of expression which gives me as much personal and professional satisfaction as the fantasies. Yet long ago when I started writing, I had not intended to finish up as a children's writer, and the dark thing at the door of my mind was still there. It had a voice, and the voice was whispering as it had many times before – why had I continued to address my historical novels to children?

Who, apart from people in the trade, took such books seriously? And so why had I not used the expertise gained from my journeyman piece and the life-time of research I had done to make people take me seriously as a writer in this line? Especially when it would have been so much easier to have cast some of my books for adults, rather than for children?

I thought of the technical problems of writing *A Pistol in Greenyards*, and the passion of feeling which had gone into that book. I thought of the one which had followed it – *The Ghosts of Glencoe* – and the even greater problems that had presented. The planned killing of the whole inhabitants of a Highland glen – how could one possibly write of that for children? The historical background to the massacre, moreover, was a highly-complicated one, peopled by men of complex character. And yet, I remembered, it was the very challenge of such difficulties which had drawn me on to write it!

Poring over the military records of the day, exploring traditional accounts of the massacre, I found hints of a situation that enabled me to assume the historical figure of Robert Stewart as a sixteen-year-old Ensign of the regiment involved. A further assumption legitimately based on the traditions of the day enabled me to place him as a stranger on the scene; and thus, through his eyes, to explain it to the reader. The very fact of his youth assumed the idealism which contrasted with the decadent brilliance of his company's Commanding Officer, and thus made it possible to draw the complex portrait required for that man. Stewart's personal involvement with victims of the massacre became the reader's involvement, replacing shock at the manner of death with pity and concern for the fact of it.

A sixteen-year-old ordered to kill stealthily and in cold blood the people who have been his friends is no different in 1692 from a youngster of similar age in our own and other centuries. The horns of his dilemma are still the same – to obey the law, or to follow his conscience. So it was Robert Stewart's agony of conscience which became the theme of the book about Glencoe. And so it became a children's book, for Stewart's agony was the universal and timeless one which lies in wait for all young people compelled to take their first look at the distorted face of the adult world.

'History is people.' I have said this often enough to adults as well as to children, and this is the sum of all my research; this is the basis of everything I have learned about the historical novel. History is ordinary people shaped and shaken by the winds of their time, as we in our time are shaped and shaken by the wind of current events. And so, to write about the people of any time, one must know them so well that it would be possible to go back and live undetected among them.

Rather than writing from the outside looking in, then, one will write from the inside looking out. Then also, as when a raised window permits interior and exterior to merge in the air and sunlight flowing into a room, the past will merge with the present. The feelings of past and present will be shared. There will be engagement between reader and characters, irrespective of superficial differences in dress, speech, and habit; and in identifying with these characters, the reader will find his own identity.

A sense of identity. This is the key phrase in considering the desired impact of a historical novel. It was at this point in my thinking that the dark shape in my mind slipped away for good. I recognized it as it went, and knew it for that very mean emotion, self-pity. I felt an impulse to laugh at my own stupidity in having so long allowed it to linger with me; for surely, I argued, achieving a sense of one's own identity is the first step towards total identification with one's environment and one's kind? And surely, also, this total identification is only a more sophisticated term for the one-to-one contact which is all that ultimately matters?

I was back with the power of human love against the soul-less ones, but approaching it roundabout by analysis, instead of directly by intuition, as in my first fantasy. I was examining the component parts of this power – courage, compassion, humility, a passionate militancy in believing the importance of truth, justice, and honesty. I was taking a fresh look at my historical novels, and realizing why – apart from the joy of following my story-teller instinct – I had continued to write them for children.

The cloak and dagger of the first two had not obscured the fact that one had been essentially about a poor man's right to justice, and that the other had been concerned with integrity. I had followed this with a much deeper exploration into the themes of courage and conscience. Similarly, in every historical novel I had written since then, I had been concerned with some aspect of this power of human love; each of these being one that a child has to learn to recognize as a component part of the whole before it can grow from its first, intuitive reliance on this power to a reasoned alliance with it.

A caring alliance too, for loving implies caring. And caring, by its very nature, is something which stretches into the future as well as covering the present. Yet how can one care about the present unless one understands it; how understand the present without a sense of the past on which it is based? How, without a sense of the whole time-continuum of past, present, and future, achieve that contact which is all that ultimately matters?

Equally, with such a simple message to impart, how could I address my historical novels to those already lost in all the twists and guilts and deformations of the adult world? I had no interest in the crowns-and-cleavage school of writing, or in racy, sub-professorial sequences of bed-battle-bed. I could think of nothing more boring than presenting a painting-by-numbers panoramic view of a period, unless it was the repetition of a sure-to-sell formula as before.

I was interested only in trying to write well enough to tell a good story; in dipping into any period of history at will, and coming back from the experience having expressed something of my own philosophy of life. These were precisely what my historical novels for children had given me opportunity to do, and so what reason had *I* to feel sorry for myself?

We have in Scotland a saying which runs: *There's a providence looks after bairns, fools, and drunk men.*

The providence certainly looked after me as a twelve-year-old bairn when I pestered Mr Miller for the story of Redhouse Castle, and so was led on to the study through which I discovered my career as a writer. It took care of me in the foolish years when the dark shape haunted me, for *something* kept me following my natural bent towards writing for children. And if it looks after the drunk, it surely has some pity for the mad also, for there was a time when I was – not clinically mad – but pressured beyond the brain's endurance by a book which had to be written.

I called it *A Sound of Chariots*. I wrote it one hot summer when the rest of my world was going about its business not realizing I was exploring into the great pain of my childhood which had been the beginning of my knowledge that I would be a writer. I finished it, put it in a drawer, and lived in peace at last, with my ghosts.

Years later, this book was accidentally brought to an editor's notice, and considered by her to be a children's book. Yet I had never thought of it as such, for writing it had involved me in total recall of that childhood pain. Processing this into a book had strained my personal and professional capacities almost to breaking point; and vaguely I felt that after all this agony I might have written something which would one day be considered notable.

So it was, in this editor's opinion – a notable children's book.

I re-read the manuscript for the first time in all those years, and saw also for the first time how I had unconsciously demonstrated there what I had later waded through seas of reasoning to prove to myself – that I was first, last, and foremost a children's writer. For it was not an adult's remembered view of experience which came off the page, but a child's urgent view of living that experience.

With relief then, I realized how well the providence had looked after me, for although it was clearly a children's book, it was clearly also one which could never have been published as such unless there had been a revolution in children's writing during the years it lay hidden. But the revolution had taken place, and my other books had allowed me to take part in it! With shame also, however, as reviewers confirmed the editor's opinion, I recalled the foolish years; for the lesson had long been writ large in my mind by then, that self-pity, for a writer, is self-destruction.

There must be inward-lookingness, of course, but only in order to project outwards what one finds in one's inmost feelings; only for purposes of identifying in that projection with one's fellow human beings. And with that God – whatever face he wears – with whom we must all finally seek to identify, or be ever held in thrall to the soulless ones.

Gather round then, children, for you are the beginning of each fresh attempt to identify and there is a story moving in my mind. And ghost – lordly ghost of Redhouse Castle! Look back at me for a moment over that shadowy shoulder. You gave me the first impulse to make my own attempt; and for this, dear murdering ghost, I owe you much thanks.

# 19

# WRITING A BOOK:
## *A DOG SO SMALL*

### *Philippa Pearce*

I ONCE wrote a story about a boy who wanted a dog. Very roughly, I took a year to think it out, a year to get it down properly on paper. In 1962 it was published as a book; and not long afterwards the BBC decided to use it on sound radio, as part of a Schools series called *Listening and Writing*. Listening children heard stories and poems, and heard fiction-writers and poets talking about how they tackled their work; the idea was to encourage children to write for themselves. So I was asked to preface the serial adaptation of my story with some account of how it came to be written.

The memory of the writing of the book was still fresh in my mind. I could recollect in detail some of the processes, and I could draw general conclusions. So I put down on paper, for speaking into a microphone, some of the things I thought significant. The piece was called *Writing a Book*. Now, years later, I still find that these recollections and generalizations ring true.

So I repeat now what I said then. Not word for word, because now the writing is for readers instead of listeners (there is less of the friendly 'you' and more of the bowler-hatted 'one'), and for adults instead of children (I can no longer assume – alas! – that story-tellers are waiting only to be encouraged, only to be liberated). But the substance is the same. I make only one change: I still believe, of course, that 'the idea of a story springs from your experience – from what you have seen and heard and done and felt and thought, going back for weeks, months, perhaps years – perhaps even to the day you were born'. But nowadays I am inclined to think that such an idea may come from before birth itself.

Here – with that exception – is what I thought about the writing of a certain story, and the writing of any story; what I still believe.

A book that is worth writing – that the writer really cares about – is only partly *made*. One may be able to make all the parts hold neatly and strongly together, as a carpenter does a good job on a box; but, before that, from the very beginning – perhaps before there is any conscious intention of writing a story – the story must *grow*. An idea grows in the mind, as a tree grows from a seed; it develops with the slowness of natural growth.

The idea of a story springs from experience – from what had been seen and heard and done and felt and thought, going back for weeks, months, perhaps years – perhaps even to birth, or earlier. To say exactly where an idea sprang from may be very difficult; it's much easier to mark its growth – its gaining in strength and in size, and its branchings out. That's what I shall do for one particular story: mine. My concern will be mostly with growth and the encouragement of growth – the cultivation, as a gardener would say; but there will also be something about making, as a carpenter makes. Growth and making can go on together, as long as the second is never allowed to interfere with the first.

Ideas for stories aren't always easily identifiable. One needs to be on the watch, to recognize them; in the beginning, they may not look like stories at all. My idea didn't look like a story; it looked like a person – a boy who longed to have a dog. It began with the longing itself, and at first that was all I knew of the boy. I never did know – and never bothered to wonder – what exactly he looked like: what colour his hair was, or his eyes, whether he was tall or short for his age, or even exactly what his age was. I didn't care about the boy's appearance because I started knowing him from the inside – what he wanted, his thoughts, his feelings; so there was no need to look at him from the outside, as you do with a stranger passing in the street. I knew that at the very centre of that boy – at the heart of him – was his longing for a dog. That was my idea for the story, and from that the boy grew, and the story grew round him, because what he wanted and what he was caused the story.

The idea grew in my mind. The boy's longing was intense – so intense that at last it created what it could not have: the boy imagined a dog for himself. He became absorbed in a waking dream of a dog more wonderful than any flesh-and-blood dog could ever be. The dream couldn't last for ever, so later the boy was alone again, without even an imaginary dog, but with the old longing. Yet that wasn't the end of the story, I was sure, although I didn't yet know what the end would be.

Now, as soon as the boy existed in my mind as a presence, as somebody there, I began trying out different scenes and scenery behind him. Some fitted, some didn't. This was like carpenter's work – fitting the right pieces together, so that they would hold. I tried the boy out, for instance, in various kinds of family and house and district. Only this suited him: a large family living in a pokey house in a back street of London. In the family, the boy had two younger brothers, who did everything together, and two elder sisters, who did everything together; and so my boy, in the middle, was always on his own, and lonely. That was why he longed for a dog, as a companion. But he couldn't have one, because the house was too small, and without any garden, and there was too much traffic in his part of London. Note that in the finished story it seems as if the boy began to long for a dog *because* he belonged to that family, and as if he couldn't have a dog *because* he lived in that house and that district. But, in fact, in my imagining of the story, the exact opposite happened: that family, house, and district were the result of the boy's hopeless longing. They were the only ones that really fitted it.

I tried out different scenes for the boy, some of them only glimpses, others complete scenes, as in a film. One of the scenes that came to me earliest of all was set on Hampstead Heath, late one summer evening. I know the Heath well, and that's when I like it best. Perhaps that was why I put my boy there then. For, when everyone else had gone home, he was still wandering on the Heath; he was the only thing you could see moving in the failing light. There was absolute stillness, too, until he called to somebody or something. I liked the dramatic way his voice cracked the silence. Then there was an answering sound from over the Heath – a dog barking, and out of the dusky distance a dog rushed towards him – a living dog for him alone. The boy and his dog met, overjoyed, and then they went over the Heath together, their shapes melting into the dusk again. And that, I realized, was the end of my story.

So, long before I had the beginning of the story, I had the end – and that was an encouragement, almost a promise. From the first, the end was there as a landmark, a destination to be aimed at.

All the same, this end that I had found asked more questions than it answered. It answered one big question: Did the boy ever get the real dog he longed for? Yes. But it asked others: Where did this dog come from? How did the Heath come into the story? How could the boy have a dog now, and not earlier? Difficult questions, that gave trouble later. Already I looked ahead towards them with anxiety: they appeared as big gaps in the story; and as well as these gaps, there was no beginning. A story without a beginning doesn't look much of a story.

This is just the time when a writer can feel stuck. He may want to give up altogether in despair; or he may feel he'd be justified in *making* the story work out – in forcing it, as one might force a lock. But I believe that forcing can be just as fatal to a story – to the life of a story – as giving up. The life of my story was in the boy, in his longing. Everything had either to grow naturally from that, or be made to fit it, as the family, house and district had been made to fit. The boy himself must never be forced to do anything. If I'd begun doing that, the boy would have become a dummy boy, to be moved about in a dead story.

For me, the important thing at this stage was to wait – to think about the story only when I wanted to; and even then not to think hard, not to reason, but to let the mind rove freely, almost lazily. In any bit of time when one hasn't positively to be thinking of something else, the mind can be wandering about in a half-grown story, exploring its possibilities.

Gradually falling asleep or waking up, dozing – these are often useful times. Sleepiness and sleep free the mind to try out possibilities that might otherwise seem too bizarre; but one of them may fit, or lead to another that fits. You can half-dream the answers to questions.

I've said that you can't force the story along, or you'll almost certainly kill it, or kill that particular part of it. But you can feed its growth. There'll be things that you suddenly remember from long ago, or things you've always known, or things you notice freshly – incidents and details from personal experience. All these you can try out in a story, hoping to nourish its growth. So the alert, observant part of your mind, the part that notices what goes on round you, can be useful in the story, as well as the part that is meditative, half-dreaming.

Noticing and remembering what had been noticed – these eventually helped me to find the missing beginning of my story. Up to then I had only the end – on Hampstead Heath – and rather a misty middle, which was the boy imagining a dog for himself. I had nothing earlier than that middle, and so I had to work backwards from that. Three things I had seen or heard took me backwards to a beginning.

First of all, up from my memory came something I had noticed in the Greenwich Naval Museum several years before. A section of the Museum was devoted to Nelson, and – as well as all the relics of sea-battles – there was a pretty bronze brooch or medallion of a dog. The label said that this had belonged to Nelson's daughter, when she was no more than an infant. Her father had promised to give her whatever she chose as a present, and she had asked for a dog. But he thought – or perhaps he was persuaded – that a dog was too rough a pet for so young a child. So, to keep his promise, and yet not to keep it, he gave her the representation of a dog in bronze. As I read the explanatory label in the Museum, I thought how bitterly disappointed – perhaps furiously angry – the little girl must have been. Now, years later, with my story growing in my mind, I thought of this again. I wondered what had happened next, for the little girl. Did she go on longing for a dog, as my boy did? And if so . . .

The story of the brooch seemed to fit with the story of the boy and his longing. But the fit couldn't be exact – for one thing, a brooch couldn't be a present for a boy.

Then came the second thing – or rather, it had been there all the time: a little, old-fashioned picture of a dog, embroidered in wool, hanging on the wall in my own home. I had seen it every day for years, but now suddenly I saw it inside the story. The picture might do instead of a brooch.

Lastly, while all this was drifting around in my mind, I happened to have a conversation with a friend, about seeing with your eyes shut. You can often remember the look of a thing more exactly if you close your eyes. And if you have been staring at something very intently, and then shut your eyes, you seem to see with peculiar vividness. And so on . . .

As that conversation continued, I seemed to hear a click in my mind, like the sound of a key turning in a lock, opening something. At last I saw the way through, that my story could go, naturally, without any forcing.

Now I could find a way back from the middle of the story, which I knew, to the missing beginning. In the middle of the story, the boy was imagining a dog. Suppose he saw this imaginary dog only when he had his eyes shut . . . Yes; and suppose this vision came in the first place from staring at a picture of a dog – a picture perhaps like the woolwork picture. He owned the picture – but wait a minute: he didn't want to own a picture of a dog; he wanted to own a real dog. Yes, but that could be the whole point – as it had been with Nelson's little daughter. The boy wanted a real dog, and he was given the representation of a dog instead. That would be a bitter disappointment, if he'd actually been promised a dog as a present – say, on his birthday.

I was there. I had travelled backwards from the middle of the story to what could be rather a good beginning: the boy's birthday, and his expecting a dog.

Finding myself there, at the beginning of the story, I wanted to start writing at once. I knew there were gaps in the story ahead, particularly towards the end. There was some mistiness elsewhere, as well; but both the gaps and the mistiness were a good way ahead. So I didn't let them deter me. I don't believe in putting off writing if one really wants to, even if everything isn't fully planned. After all, one can pause for days, if necessary, between stretches of writing – between chapters, probably – and think ahead again. And if things do go wrong, one can go back afterwards and put them right. That may be a nuisance, but it's less dangerous than putting off writing when one feels ready. The danger then would be that one might forget what was at the tip of one's pen – that one might lose the excitement that often leads to the best writing.

So I started on the first chapter. The story fell into chapters as I went along, and it was only occasionally that I was in doubt where exactly to make a chapter end. In the finished story there were nearly twenty chapters, but long before I could foresee that, I had begun to see that the story was going into a natural pattern of three big sections. These were made by the three different dogs the boy had, one after the other: first, the woolwork picture of a dog; second, the imaginary dog; third, the living dog that came over Hampstead Heath.

The end of the first section – the woolwork dog – actually overlapped a little with the beginning of the next section – the imaginary dog that the boy saw with his eyes shut. This overlap came in the middle of a chapter. I wrote that chapter with particular excitement, because I felt myself at a turning point of the story. After that, the story would be really growing, as a young tree grows, according to its nature – the nature which I had given it. A phrase of dialogue at that turning point also gave me the title for the story when it was finished: *A Dog so Small.*

# 20

# WRITING A BOOK:
# *GOODNIGHT, PROF, LOVE*

## *John Rowe Townsend*

WRITING a book is a job of work. For me it is hard work: harder than any other kind of work I've ever done. After it's finished I can enjoy the luxury of rationalizing about it: finding an explanation of why it was written at all, why it came out the way it did, what it is supposed to be saying, and to whom. But when I am actually writing I am, above all else, fighting with the material: fighting and fighting, losing some days, winning others, going back and fighting again, never triumphant but usually reaching a stage where I feel I have done the best I could. I don't have time while writing to worry too much about how the readers will react, although I suppose that somewhere around the shadowy borders of my mind is a shadowy audience consisting of myself when young and my own children and my children's friends. My aim is simply to write the books I have it in me to write, and to make as good a job of them as I can.

Probably the most interesting thing an author has to tell anyone else is what went on while a book was being written. Unfortunately, recollections after the event are not always reliable. It happens however that I have pretty full records of work on most of my books, made while it was actually in progress. This is because the only way I can work is to sit at the typewriter and put my thoughts on to paper as they occur. I would like to be able to build books in my head while travelling or gardening or doing housework, but it's no good; if I don't get my ideas straight down in typescript they simply evaporate.

So before I start writing a book I try to get a rough plan of it on paper; while I'm writing it I address constant memoranda to myself about people, places and incidents; and whenever I'm stuck – which happens quite often – I make a fresh attempt to work out on paper the way ahead from whatever point I'm stuck at.

The result is that when I have finished the book I am left with a sheaf of notes-along-the-way. Three-quarters of them relate to the wrenching out from myself of a rough draft: that part of writing which is accomplished by what Arnold Bennett called 'brute force of brain'. Having made a rough draft, I try to analyse it and work out how it can best be beaten into shape; after that there are notes on the second draft and on the final revision. But in these later stages the work grows less difficult and the notes briefer; craftsmanship begins to become enjoyable, the problems feel as if they can be solved. For me the last revision is the best part of writing a book; if all has gone well it's like coming safely into port after a long voyage. But I don't ever want to make the same journey twice.

What follow are extracts from the notes I made while writing a book called *Goodnight, Prof, Love,* published in 1970. I have chosen it because it was a fairly short and straightforward book, and the notes are not too extensive or complicated. Even so, I have had to shorten them a good deal. I have tried not to falsify by selective omission; and so far as I know the only way in which these extracts might mislead is in not indicating sufficiently that I often headed up blind alleys and had to turn back. The book took about four months to write, which for me is extremely good going. (Its predecessor, *The Intruder,* took a year and a half, which is much more usual.) It happens that *Goodnight, Prof, Love* is more what the Americans call a 'young adult', i.e. teen-age, novel rather than a children's book; but so far as my methods of writing are concerned there is no important difference.

As these are working notes, they tend to deal with practical problems. They put more emphasis on plotting and the organization of material, a little less on characterization, and much less on style and atmosphere, than I would if I were trying to indicate the relative importance of these aspects of a book.

*Idea for possible book*                              *11 September 1969*

The obsessive passion of a boy of about sixteen for a somewhat older and more experienced girl. His name – Graham. A quiet studious boy. He wants to earn money and gets a job at Mac's Transport Café, part-time; falls hook line and sinker for a blonde waitress whom he endows with various virtues but who is really no better than she should be. She's flattered by her conquest, because he's brainier than any boy who's chased her in the past; at the same time she's contemptuous of his innocence and inexperience.

Graham sees her as a flower on a dunghill; is determined to get her out of it. Thinks he'll take her to Gretna and marry her. Perhaps this appeals to her as a joke. And they run off together; stow away in the back of a lorry.

They are pursued by his father, chased into some corner. Up in the hills somewhere. Graham nearly does violence to his father, but the girl prevents him. Later she tells him it's all off, she was never serious. On the way home in the car Father says he *bought* her off. At home, Mother pitches into him. Father vaguely restraining, Graham won't say a word. But there's blood on his lip where bitten.

Uncertain yet [i.e. uncertain in the author's mind] whether Father really bought her off or not. An important question, linking with this, will be whether the experience is a constructive or a destructive one for Graham. Presumably the former, which would imply that the girl has good qualities.

This would be a short book, single-minded, pursuing the one theme. It would need unity of mood, economy, great intensity, and ideally a special style to match the obsessional intensity.

*More thoughts on next book*        *16–18 September 1969*

Basic characters:

*The boy.* Graham. He lives in a town like Macclesfield. Tall, fair-haired, spectacled, conscientious, maybe sets clock daily for early work. A poor mixer, has never had a girl-friend.

*Father.* Small-town accountant, competent, reasonably worldly-wise (has seen quite a bit of human nature professionally). Practises as 'and Son', and takes it for granted that Graham will be articled to him when he leaves school.

*Mother.* Emotional, a bit in love with her son, though she doesn't realize it; would certainly be jealous of the girl, as well as frightened of her for Graham's sake.

*The girl.* Her name could be Lynn, adapted from Linda, but at this stage it doesn't matter. She left school at fifteen, has a family somewhere around Birmingham but doesn't bother with them or they with her. She's maybe eighteen, sexually casual but not vicious. Has warmth, generosity, more to her in many ways than at first appears; an *unfolding* character, already formed, whereas Graham will be developing rapidly under stress. She'll probably get quite fond of him (and I of her) before we've finished.

*Café proprietor.* Jeff? 35–38ish, single or separated, drinks a lot of beer and looks it, but not exactly a drunkard, in fact likes to appear more drunk than he really is. Lynn could be living with him, but this wouldn't at first sink in with Graham and might not sink in with an innocent reader.

The 'stone in the pool' that sets things moving is a row between Lynn and Jeff, which results in her having nowhere to go. And Graham takes her home. Of course his parents object. But they give her a bed in the spare room.

Next day they're all set to put her on the train (for Birmingham, where her family live). But she doesn't intend to go. Tells Graham she'll go back to Jeff, who will have sobered up by now. But G. can't bear the thought of that. He comes out with his plan to go to Gretna Green and get married. Maybe the episode is also making him desperate to get away from his parents. (Mother could be *very* unpleasant about Lynn.) She agrees, seeing it as a bit of a lark.

Graham leaves her at station, goes home, tells mother he is walking over moors to his aunt's; this enables him to pack a rucksack without arousing suspicion. Goes back into town more determined than ever. Next problem: even if *he* hasn't changed his mind, won't she have done so by now? Well, maybe, maybe not. She's had enough of Jeff, really. She could propose tossing a coin or anything to indicate how impulsive her actions are. And they're off.

I think there are two stops on the journey. They are hitching. The first stop is at a place like Blackpool [must go there soon]. They arrive at the pleasure beach, eat, go on a lot of rides, spend quite lavishly, boy sick and dizzy, they book in at a grandiosely named but crummy little hotel, a bedroom scene but nothing actually happens. Next day a truck driver offers them a lift as far as Cobchester [Manchester]. But perhaps they go from place-like-Blackpool to Cobchester on the train; this avoids having three successive hitches.

They could go to Gumble's Yard. After a while Lynn gets restless, goes off somewhere, comes back with grinning friend who'll take them up to Scotland.

Could be that the girl herself would betray Graham – not necessarily maliciously. Anyway at some stage – perhaps at a place-like-Shap – they find themselves at the wayside and along comes Father (or Father comes with Jeff). Then as in previous note.

Later G. goes round to the *caff* again and she's there, back with Jeff, fairly unconcerned. Admits having taken money; sees it as a bonus, not easily come by. 'You want to grow up,' she tells him. Which of course is the right advice, and she hasn't behaved specially badly. His bitterness could be passing already. He has torn up his photograph of her; now he recovers it, pastes it together, and there she is again, though not quite the same. Could be that he sets the clock for morning. End.

*Blackpool pleasure beach visit*               *Saturday night 20 September 1969*

Very crowded; practically everything open and doing lots of business; promenade outside packed for the illuminations, cars, trams, coaches crawling along (but hardly anyone on the pier). Standard of behaviour good while I was there, prices of rides and refreshments seemed reasonable – all quite decent, innocent and enjoyable. Long queues for most popular rides. Big dipper and several other big things; log-run the most interesting. And the Monster – a horrible octopod contraption with writhing limbs of virulently coloured lights. The laughing man still around – apparently a king now. And the ghost train. Some for the kids – Noah's Ark, Alice. Hats with slogans – SOCK IT TO ME, BABY; BOY WANTED – no experience needed. Rifle ranges; a football game where the kind of lads who kick balls around can kick balls around, aiming at knockdown figures of well-known footballers, or (small in foreground) the nervous bespectacled ref. A rather fine roundabout with galloping horses. Dodgems. Remarkable number of arcades full of penny-catching machines and pin-tables, some time-honoured. But they must be the only thing that hasn't gone up since the 1930s. And a maze with plateglass and mirrors (could be a symbolic scene here). The well-known thin wails as the dippers go down or the Monster down-and-round. Girls' hair flying out. A late-thirtyish woman on her own, round innocent slightly-worn face, enjoying herself. Lots of refreshment places, but (I think) nothing alcoholic. Imagine reeling back to your boarding house, head spinning and ringing, your whole being happily full of light and sound and movement, hot dogs and fizzy drinks whirling amicably together in your stomach.

Soon afterwards I drafted a first chapter in which Graham, taking his dog for a walk, passes Jeff's Café just as the girl runs out, pursued by Jeff. Graham helps her to get away, she tells him she has nowhere to go, and he takes her to his parents' house. But this, I felt, was not satisfactory.

### *More thoughts on next book*        *10 October 1969*

The drafted first chapter was all very well to get started but will not really do. It is altogether too foreshortened. We need to get to know Graham, the girl, Jeff, the parents as well perhaps, before things start moving. Graham's obsession needs to be seen growing. The town also requires to be built up. Let's consider the beginning again. We have to get Graham into Jeff's. He's a solitary, a daydreamer. His parents would not worry too much about leaving him in the house while they went away for a few days. He could have food, money for meals, and that would take him to Jeff's. Daydreaming all the way and also bored. And the girl would take his eye. She might deliberately flirt with him a bit, with half an eye on Jeff, with whom she's having a bit of a tiff (over extra duties perhaps). This is where he sees the possibility of a job. And gets taken on. Actually the girl is ready to break with Jeff and things are getting strained between them. Graham stands up for her. He has been labelled 'the Prof'. She thinks he's clever; has a half-genuine half-contemptuous admiration for him. In fact her flirting could become quite outrageous, and as we've said the poor lad becomes besotted. After a few days there's a great big row. And he takes her to his house. And back come his parents. And from then on as in 'More thoughts' of 16–18 September. First draft of first chapter pretty well written off.

### *Thoughts on Chapter 4 in rough draft*        *undated*

We're taking a long time to get to the beginning of the real action. But the characters are building up quite nicely. Maybe the first three chapters will have to be tightened up, and any repetitions or near-repetitions removed.

This chapter must get as far as the parents' return to find Lynn in the house. Which gives us a fair amount of psychological distance to cover. (This really is why the opening chapters have extended themselves and the first draft of all would not do.) Seems reasonable that Graham should now start falling for her pretty rapidly, since she is there in flesh and blood against the competition of mere imaginings. This has to be indicated. Tuesday night the girl is out with Jeff. Wednesday she is back again, perhaps more attentive to Graham than ever, perhaps now confiding in him that she's fed up with Jeff. At the end of that night Graham gets sacked. Thursday he's loafing around in a total whirl; this perhaps is the day in which his obsession with Lynn really takes hold. Friday he goes down to the caff, is hanging around, hoping to see her, and she comes dashing out, taking refuge with him.

*Goodnight, Prof, Love*                                     *4 November 1969*

[This was the point at which the book began to have a title. It suggested itself when the phrase was used by Lynn in the last line of what became Chapter Three of the final version.]

Where do we go from p. 71 in the rough draft? Problem: how to get Lynn and Graham on the road. First: do we have a night visit to Graham from Mother? Might be a good idea to try it and see how it works out. Then the morning. I think Lynn is fast asleep, then a bit surly, bad-tempered. Father drives them to the station. He offers Lynn money which she refuses ungraciously. A scene in station concourse. This must be where Graham comes up with his proposition. I think it has to grow on them. They talk themselves into the idea gradually. They are discovering a fondness for each other. G. will go home for his money and his bank book; and his mother, thinking he's going for a lone walk on the moors (like his old self) packs him sandwiches. He's not at all sure that Lynn will still be there. But she is. She's waiting for him, eager. They get the bus to the far side of town, then a lift to the motorway in a van driven by a pal of Lynn's. On the motorway it takes time to get a further lift, and when they do, Lynn's in the front of a truck and G. behind. Not having slept much the night before, he could easily fall asleep and not wake up till they're at Pool.

The question of Mother: how far to develop her as a character? This is the story of Graham and Lynn, not an imitation of *Sons and Lovers*; which would suggest keeping Mother in the background, playing scenes 'off' her (like the discovery scene), while *implying* that she is emotional, possessive, the cause of much trouble both in and for Graham. Which in turn suggests that she should not actually appear in a night scene; we should merely have Graham's consciousness that she will be lying awake. Perhaps this should be stressed two or three times, not only in the brief Graham/Lynn night scene, so that throughout this chapter the reader has an awareness of the unsleeping woman in the other bedroom.

*Goodnight, Prof, Love*                                        *16 November 1969*

From p. 110, end chapter nine in rough draft: Lynn and Graham are in bed and asleep in a scruffy backstreet Pool-on-Sea boarding house. There are three more stages of their travels: to Gumble's Yard, to a place-like-Shap near the border, and home. It's Saturday morning. The wave-pattern of the story would suggest that it's now time for wet weather, for them to fall out, for things to start going wrong. At G.Y. it will clear up, they'll be happy and at home, they'll make love, they'll set out bright and gay for Gretna Green. And, near the border, Nemesis.

It seems to be settled that the whole thing is seen from within or behind Graham. This rules out any scenes back in the home town. But the parents and Jeff are not to be forgotten. The only ways of keeping them in mind are those being used throughout: either dialogue or stream-of-thought. Perhaps it's better done by dialogue, since G. will be able to speculate on his parents and L. in turn to speculate on Jeff; *but* it would be a good lead-in for the next chapter if G. were churning this over in his head before L. wakes.

When L. does wake she'll be snappy and he'll go down to breakfast alone. And fail to get her a cup of tea, for which she tells him off. She could send him out on to the promenade for cigarettes, and he bumps into his Uncle Roger, taking the dog for a walk. It's a wet day. Does Uncle R. already know he's gone—or, a possibility, does G. merely jump to the conclusion that he does? Is he even sure it's actually Uncle Roger he sees?

Anyway, back he goes to Lynn, who is now inclined for dalliance. But he is in a panic, and wants to be off. They take the train, so as to get out of town quickly, and go to seek Lynn's former girl friend in Cobchester. For some reason she is not available, but they are near Gumble's Yard, and Lynn knows about it (reason required). The sky is clearing now, they are having fun, scuffling, setting up a pretend home, and all is well. And so today they make love.

Next day is Sunday and they lie in. Sunshine coming in through those grimy windows (unless we needed it the previous day). But eventually they will, or at least she will, want to go into town, for a meal or the cinema or something. And now they meet Sam Bell, [a truck driver] who definitely does know that she's left Jeff and that Jeff wants her back. He appears to be on their side, but is a traitor. It's possible that Lynn, with good or at least ambiguous intentions, is conniving at treachery; consider. (A dash of colour needed in the settings: could the meal and the betrayal be in an expensive restaurant, or anyway somewhere fairly exotic?)

Sam offers them a ride in his truck. High road over the moors; heather. Graham's spirits rising as they near the promised land. But near the border Sam professes to have engine trouble, and stops and keeps them talking at the wayside until the appearance of Jeff and/or Mr Hollis (Graham's father).

*Goodnight, Prof, Love*                                        *21 November 1969*

Now, how to finish it off?

Not the trip back, not the confrontation with Mother. But a quiet scene with Father. He'll say, 'Can't you imagine the state your mother's been in?' And of course Graham can, and so can we, so we don't need to see it. Mother is to be told that 'nothing happened' between G. and the girl. The great question – how did Father know where they were? Well, Lynn telephoned. Father and Jeff decided to do it this way rather than try to pick Graham up in broad daylight in the middle of Cobchester. But why did she do it? G. wants to know. She sold you, says Father. 'She sold you, Graham, for fifty pounds, cash down. I hope you feel you're worth it.'

Graham is sort-of reconciled to his parents. But later Father shows him the money, returned through the post; admits he wasn't quite frank. She didn't ask for the money; he offered her it; she refused at first, then took it and said, 'Tell him I took it'. Father hasn't actually lied, but the impression given was wrong. He is touched now, being an honest man, and says so: 'Everything in order and above board, that's what we insist on in our profession. And now it applies to this little matter, too. So can we draw a line under it, eh, son? Account closed?' 'I guess so, Dad. Account closed.'

But there'll have to be a final Graham soliloquy in which he sees that in her way she did love him. (She returned him to his parents for his own good.)

– I might see her again some time.

– You won't.

– I'll not marry anyone else.

–You will.

– All right. Finished now. The end of the day. Settle down, don't worry. Goodnight, Prof. Goodnight, Lynn, love. God bless.

[This, give or take a word or two, is how the book did actually end.]


*Thoughts on the first draft*                    *11 December 1969*

Well, there's something there. Now to apply some intelligence, so far as available, to its further shaping.

The theme really is responsibility in personal relationships, or rather, the moral concern is that. But that's hindsight. It's the story of Graham and Lynn.

The action seems satisfactory. The time-scale is on the short side – all that really matters happens within nine days – but this is within the tolerances of the novel form. The story divides clearly into two halves; they could even be 'part one' and 'part two'. The first half builds towards a three-stepped climax: Lynn's walking out on Jeff, the return of Graham's parents to find her with him, and the decision to elope. (Diminuendo in this half has been Graham's daydream, a girl of air rather than flesh and blood.) The second half deals with the elopement itself. The first half covers six days, the second, three. This distribution seems about right. The geographical movement also seems fair enough.

The first-half climax needs dramatically pointing-up, however. And while Lynn is clearly at a turning-point, we need to be convinced that Graham is enough in love, and/or sufficiently desperate, finding home life sufficiently intolerable, to take this drastic step.

The second half also needs a dramatic pattern, which possibly it doesn't have. There is constant hesitation; a sense from the start that this enterprise is not going to get anywhere; and this must tend towards anticlimax. The pattern required is surely (i) initial impetus; (2) reaction; (3) renewed impetus; (4) suspense; (5) disaster. Where these come in the story is obvious, but once again they need pointing-up. Graham cannot be allowed his perpetual doubts; he can at most have one attack of cold feet. There mustn't be all the havering there is in the first draft; we must feel that they could get somewhere, that Graham believes in the enterprise and hopes to be happy.

Form: at present, narrative gradually diminishes, and the second half is almost entirely dialogue and interior-monologue. This is not necessarily a bad pattern. It might be worth experimenting to see if the whole thing could be done the second way, but the result could be forbidding. Better perhaps to ease the reader into it gradually, as in this draft.

Characters: Graham and Lynn are the ones that really matter, and if they're not right now they never will be, so it's no good worrying about them. The only other characters who count are G.'s parents, Jeff, Sam Bell and Alice [a woman who works in the cafe]. Jeff and Alice are all right. Sam, having met two different functional demands, is in two pieces but can be put together again on the rewrite. The major problem is with the parents. If the subject of the story were G.'s relationship with *them*, or his growing up over a period of time, then they would be very prominent and would have to be developed in depth and portrayed at some length. But the subject of the story is G.'s elopement with Lynn. An extended treatment of the parents could clog the action, blur the dramatic line. This suggests, what indeed has actually happened, that they will be drawn more simply and sharply than one would really wish. What's needed is, perhaps, not a careful rounding but a touch here and there to show that they're human, decent, not stock figures.

There, in effect, my working notes on *Goodnight, Prof, Love* ended. There were a few brief notes on points that arose in rewriting, but they are of no great interest. There is no assessment of the finished book. Once a book is as good as the author can make it, it is no longer his business, and he should be getting on with something else.

I think that what the reader gets from the book has a very oblique and uncertain relationship to what the author put in. The reader draws out what he wants and needs, and perhaps what he gets is related mainly to what he himself puts in. Readers often assume however that a more direct effect is intended. I had a letter, not long after *Goodnight, Prof, Love* was published, from a boy of sixteen who asked what it was 'intended to mean' and what my motives were in writing it. He'd liked it but was puzzled. I said, 'I don't think *Goodnight, Prof, Love* is intended to "mean" anything in the sense of making an important statement about life. Basically it is a story, which I hope is interesting, about people, who I hope are interesting. If it is true to human nature, then inferences about human nature can be drawn from it; but that's a matter for the reader. The author doesn't necessarily understand better than the reader what his book is about.'

# 21

# THE THORNY PARADISE
## Barbara Willard

To write about writing is somehow a tough assignment. For better or worse, writing is a craft almost without rules – apart from the basics of word building you can make up everything else as you go along and settle for the way that best suits you. No one can ever rebuke: 'That is not the way to do it,' for quick as light comes the reply: 'It is the right way for me.'

This book is about approaches to writing for children, which I find rather daunting. There are many variations on such a theme – approach through plot, approach through characters, through style, even. Some writers in this field do indeed have a purpose, moral, educative, and these are the ones who should best be able to explain themselves. One can better be specific about approaches *to* authors, and see where that leads. Who do you write for? one is asked. That means: Do you write for your own children/grandchildren/godchildren? How can you write for more than one age group? I have often been asked this myself. It is a question that will always leave me at a loss; some stories are about six-year-olds, and some are about sixteen-year-olds – one takes what comes and is grateful. Why don't you write really short, really gripping stories in a limited vocabulary for slow readers? . . . These approaches can make for rather gritty reactions, and it is now that the author will reply, snappishly or cringingly – 'I write for myself.' If authors give their questioners such sharp replies, it is often because they are backing away uneasily from what seems, however well intentioned, an intrusion. What are you working on now? is another horror, since it is quite possible to talk a tale out of exist-ence. A tale is for telling; and all too often, once it is discussed and de-scribed, it is indeed told, so that there may seem little reason for the effort of writing it down. This is a very saddening experience.

In fact, however one shies away, why do you write? who do you write for? what is your approach? are questions that set one's sense of respon-sibility twitching, and therefore they must be valuable. The whole writing business is very hard to assess – too basic to be jeered at, too mundane to be treated reverently. Writers write because they want to – most probably they have no other gifts, anyway. One might say the stripped-down motive is sheer self-indulgence. If, in doing what he most wants to do, a writer also scratches himself a living, then indeed he may contrive his own life-style within a kind of thorny paradise. Others doing what are called proper jobs understandably treat such wastrels with the contempt born of envy. This is because they know nothing of those thorns; the awful vacancies, the lonely wrestling, the disappointments – disappointments of ability most of all; the grinding realization that you are not quite up to your own ideas, that you are obliged, weakly, to find a way round . . . Survival is assured only by the reverse of this coin, which must have spun at least once for every author – the story that springs fully-armed, peopled, shaped and inevitable – the story that you can *hear*. 'I have finished *The School for Scandal*,' Sheridan reputedly said. 'It has only to be written.'

Approaches from the young offer their own delights.

'How old were you,' a boy of nine or so asked me, 'when your first book was published?'

I had been about twenty, I said. He gave me a long, but not unkind look. 'You must have written an awful lot since then,' he said.

It's not all just jokey, though. Once young readers have discovered that books are not prefabricated, but are the work of living, breathing, crying, laughing men and women, they are full of curiosity. They have a vision of their authors then, it seems, as a distant band working in isolation in a strange, slightly magical world, where all are easily rich and famous. 'But she can't be!' one girl said to a young relation of mine who had, with some embarrassment, pointed me out. 'I saw her out *shopping*!' In fact when they see us displaying ourselves at school and library functions, I often think they must be pretty dashed to find us ordinary, puzzled, self-doubting and self-engrossed. But such confrontations are utterly salutary for the authors, and would be so if only because practical questions often show up error – 'Why did you write This on page twelve, and That on page twenty-one?' But there is more – the comfort of 'I know you really knew what the hero was thinking, because that's how I should think,' and the challenge of great diversity in the questioning. They may start with inquiries about the number of pages, the number of words, but some of them are ambitious enough to suggest that here is a writer in embryo.

But however they veer and vary, they always come at some point to the author-character relationship. I know that I wait for this, that it is a question I want to answer. So I suppose I come at last to the solution of my own approach to writing for children: it is indeed through my characters.

*Which comes first,* they ask, *the plot or the people?* The people every time. It is quite possible to start on the first page knowing practically nothing about what is to happen – so long as you know who it will happen to – and still find oneself writing The End on the last page of what looks like an elegant and shapely tale. The proclivities of the characters have done the work. Or you could turn out a story beautifully plotted, logical and dramatic, never swerving from a preconceived plan and find the whole thing in a state of messy collapse – simply because of a lack of liaison with even quite a minor character. A really strong character, undisciplined, can, equally, bring havoc to the page; an over-controlled character can only present an image without a shadow. I imagine that the perfect author should be like a good chairman, handling a lively meeting with tact and firmness, giving a bit here, drawing back a bit there, keeping the whole meeting on the move without obtruding, and winding up in the time allowed on a conclusion satisfactory to all. An ideal towards which one can at least strive.

What seems to me a rather more confusing problem is the take-over by some character or characters, not so much of the story as of its author. It is quite possible to write many books happily, competently and even successfully, in the quiet confidence of a good relationship all round; but, just as in human relationships, when the so-called *real thing* occurs all else pales before the impact. This fuller relationship does not, of course, result automatically in the perfect book, any more than a perfect marriage necessarily produces perfect offspring. What does result, though, is a sort of haunting; the author becomes obsessed, single-minded, egocentric, transmuting all experience into tribute to lay at the feet of his monster.

Experience has shown me that this is an almost perilous condition. Something less than twenty years ago, moving house, I was presented with a landscape of forest and heath – my native heath, indeed – the High Weald, the remnant of the Saxon forest of Andredswald. After a good quarter of those years had passed, the landscape began to fill up. The magic of the place resolved itself into the magic of man withdrawn, of the remaining footprint that brings your heart into your throat as you look down, afraid to glance back over your shoulder. They had been here, they had gone. They had cut down trees and dug stone and left un-numbered oddments behind; particularly the remnants of an iron in-dustry that had sustained the region for hundreds of years – ditches and banks and dammed streams that fed ponds, the hammer ponds that often later became millponds, and exist now either for ornament or fishing, or simply as great stretches of reedy melancholy.

When I first wrote about this piece of country, I used it chiefly as a background to a story basically about something else. But the whole thing developed into a most terrible entanglement – for writing a second story, set some years later than the first, and using what now seemed the only possible background, I realized that the people in the first book were living not far away, that they were bound to know one another. Almost before I had taken in what was happening, the two sets of characters grew hopelessly involved with one another – in no time at all, they were inter-marrying! I had still made my approach by way of the characters; but by the end of the second book, the setting was, or seemed to me to be, equally important. These are not *historical novels* in the grand sense – I am no scholar, anyway. They could be called an attempt at putting on old clothes, seeing how they feel rather than merely looking at them in a mirror, walking in them over ground where they were once worn; but they do have to be old clothes and not fancy dress. If only one or two readers find themselves insinuated into the period in this way, then the enterprise has achieved some end.

Probably all of us writing these stories for the older young share one particular problem. They are in effect novels, and they need novel length. The characters do have some time to develop and fill in – but these are people one has time to love but must always leave too soon. The wrench can be painful. There has not been time to do the best for them. It has been impossible to tell all one knows. The one or two on the sidelines, who might have moved forward and taken a more active part – how can they ever be compensated? Perhaps it is faulty plotting to have any lurking characters at all – and yet how often one such has been waiting for a crisis, and seized the opportunity like a good understudy, and rushed in and saved the day: providing, most mysteriously, the one vital link and preserving the plot intact.

It is of course this loving and leaving that lures us into the writing of sequels. We cannot let our darlings go, and returning to them is a homecoming. Yet the re-union can be difficult. They have aged, acquired children, grandchildren whose names, even, one does not know. They have almost certainly developed prejudices they deplored in their own parents and are learning, as every generation must, to cope with their young.

Most children's writers write a lot of books, and there are many reasons for this, some of them merely practical. But one good reason is the pure pleasure of finding an uncynical audience. Stern, uncompromising, but never weary. It is a wonderful appetite to feed, that lovely maw, enticingly open. No wonder children's books proliferate and reviewers grow a bit tetchy at times. Anyway, it is suspect to be prolific, in spite of the fact that great fiction writers of the past had an enormous output.

Or perhaps it is just that fiction itself has become faintly suspect, its old respectability swallowed in the rather awful earnestness of our fact-worshipping times. And writers may be found who apologize for a mere story, and sometimes consciences are eased because the story is a problem story appropriate to the day – it will teach – help – promote understanding . . . Why not? Many a child will be helped by finding his worries rationally discussed in a fictional setting. In the same way he may be led by a story with a period setting towards a serious interest in history. Perhaps this may be called an approach – that without any ambition to *teach* young readers about themselves as they were however-many years ago, I should like to believe that this kind of story is capable of warming up history; putting the expression, in fact, into so many bald, unthinking statements that make no more impact than some common catchphrase: The Norsemen harried the coast, burning and pillaging . . . Many thousand died of the plague in that week alone . . . Unnumbered dead littered the field . . .

I have always written – we all say that; but it is mostly the case, for the bug prefers tender flesh – but never, since the first ecstasies, with as much pleasure and satisfaction as I experience today. And, as the boy recognized, I have written an awful lot by now.

# 22

# SOME INGREDIENTS OF
# *WATERSHIP DOWN*

*Richard Adams*

I PUT little trust in theory and dogma about writing for children. Walter de la Mare is credited with saying that there was no such thing as a children's book, and indeed, if there is one question that makes me feel irritable (though I hope I don't show it) it is 'What age-group is it aimed at?' (Might we have a competition to devise replies? 'I don't aim it, madam. It just goes off by itself.' 'The Ice Age group, sir.' Or, 'Well, sort of eight to eighty—', a truthful reply.) C. S. Lewis was clearly of a similar mind when he distinguished three categories of 'children's books'. The first and best, said he, is the good book which happens, almost incidentally, to be a book enjoyed by children. Whether specifically intended for children or not, such a book is, first and foremost, a work of artistic integrity, by its subject and merits appealing to readers of all ages, including children. The two 'Alice' books probably head the list here, with *The Wind in the Willows* in honourably high place; but one could, thank God, draw up a splendidly long list. *Robinson Crusoe* (unabridged), *Gulliver's Travels* (unabridged), *Mr. Midshipman Easy, Jane Eyre, The Mill on the Floss, Moonfleet, Treasure Island, Oliver Twist, A Christmas Carol, The Hobbit,* The Ghost Stories of M. R. James, *The Tale of Pigling Bland, Green Eggs and Ham, Lord of the Flies, Animal Farm, The Owl Service*; and I hope, reader, that you are now itching to shout out a few more which I have culpably omitted. What all these have in common is that the reader, of whatever age, consciously or unconsciously feels, 'This is not a book which is written down to anyone. In writing it, the author has been primarily concerned to express what he felt, and his imagination, while at work, has taken account of the nature of the world in a responsible manner. No aspect of real life has been wrongly suppressed or untruthfully left out in a way damaging to the book's integrity.' For example, in *Treasure Island* it is made quite clear that the pirates used foul language. The actual language does not need to be quoted. And the absence of any real mention of sexual matters as part of the framework of life is not out of place (as it is, rather, in *The Lord of the Rings*, to my way of thinking), because that absence is consistent with the nature of the story and with the fact that it is ostensibly being recounted by a boy. Lewis's other two categories were: the book which originated as a tale (oral or written) told to children (actually, of course, this includes *Alice in Wonderland*, *The Wind in the Willows* and others), and (the category he said he disliked) the story deliberately constructed with a view to appealing to children in general, without any particular child or children in mind. If by this he meant a children's story written in conformity with a preconceived formula or theory, I would agree. ('Leave that out – put that in – it's aimed at the ten-year-old age-group, you see!')

Only the other day I was reading an article (it was a fairly lengthy analysis of *Watership Down*, as a matter of fact, and it told me a whole lot of things I'd never dreamt of, though I don't say they were wrong) which threw out, almost *en passant*, and apparently as a truism, the remark that of course children need books which assure them of an established moral order – and this from a trendy young man, a lecturer in English at a university. For years of my childhood I found solace and delight in the poems of Walter de la Mare. These are informed throughout, in the most disturbing manner, by a deep sense of mankind's ultimate ignorance and insecurity. ('The Children of Stare' is a really frightening poem in my opinion.) De la Mare scarcely mentions Christianity – if indeed he can be said to mention it at all. Cold, ghosts, grief, pain and loss stand all about the little cocoon of bright warmth, which is everywhere pierced by a wild, numinous beauty, catalyst of fear and weeping. Why ever should this be comforting? First, I think, simply because the words, sounds and rhythms are so beautiful. John Mouldy in his cellar is beautiful in the same way as Agamemnon's dreadful death-cry from within the palace. Secondly, the poems possess and confer dignity – they make you feel, though perhaps unconsciously, that the human race is nobler and grander than you knew. (The late Mr Sidgwick, in his book, *The Promenade Ticket*, said that on Judgement Day he intended to get an orchestra and play God the Unfinished Symphony. If that didn't reconcile Him to humanity, nothing would.) Thirdly, they tell the truth. I used to weep at the grief of the Mad Prince, of poor Robin and his wife, of Dame Hickory and Mrs Gill. But I also felt that this poet treated me as a potential adult and showed respect for me by telling me the truth – and all in words of storm, rainbow and wave. His sorrow was better than Mabel Lucie Attwell's reassurance. From de la Mare I derived early the idea that one must at all costs tell the truth to children, not so much about mere physical pain and fear but about the really unanswerable things – what Thomas Hardy called 'the essential grimness of the human situation'. Later in life, I found other writers who plainly felt this equally deeply, knowing what it meant (as opposed to merely subscribing to the idea). Richard Hughes's *A High Wind in Jamaica* shows plainly enough what he feels. *Watership Down*, of course, is not a highly numinous book (as is, for example, *The Three Royal Monkeys*), but I would like to think that Silverweed, the story of the Black Rabbit and the Epilogue are in some degree in debt to the atmosphere of de la Mare's lyrics. Ultimately, of course, El-ahrairah *is* the Black Rabbit, but not in any way that we – or rabbits – can expect to comprehend in this world. But it is, perhaps, significant that Bigwig asks for the story of the Black Rabbit, to encourage him before he goes into Efrafa. He prefers the truth, as did I when a child.

My childhood – the twenties and early thirties – was the heyday of J. M. Barrie and of Christopher Robin, when children were seen by many people primarily as delicate, sensitive, small creatures, who ought properly to live in a world from which not only suffering, but to some extent reality, were excluded until they were older. This idea is not altogether false, of course, but at that time it was overdone, and in this connection I can't resist quoting Beachcomber's parody of 'When We Were Very Young'.

> I've got a silkworm
> A teeny-tiny silkworm,
> I call my silkworm
> Theobald James.
> But Nursie says it's cruel,
> Nursie says it's wicked,
> To call a little teeny-tiny silkworm names.
>
> I said to my silkworm,
> 'Oh, Mr Silkworm,
> I'd rather be a silkworm
> Than anything, far.'
> And Nursie says he answered,
> Nursie says he shouted,
> 'You wish you were a silkworm?
> You little prig, you are!'

I personally felt resentful of this general atmosphere, which thwarted one's natural aggression while at the same time unfitting one for the rougher side of life, so that one felt – and hated knowing that one was justified in feeling – at a disadvantage. An interesting expression of this difficulty is to be found in Stephen Spender's lyric, 'My parents kept me from children who were rough'. (No. XII in the 'Poems' of 1933.) It was also a time when quite a lot of people tended to tell lies to children with a view to protecting them from apprehension, fear and grief. The trouble was that the lies tended to fall down. They told you the dentist wasn't going to hurt; but of course he did. They said the cat hadn't been run over. Later, the gardener told you it had. This kind of deprivation – deprivation of the natural human lot of physical fear, pain and hardship – should, I think, be considered as something separate from deprivation of the numinous and disturbing. The latter I never really suffered. The former I certainly did – and it has not really got much to do with the latter.

In this difficulty I derived a lot of help and comfort from the books of Ernest Thompson Seton. He didn't dodge danger, fear, bloodshed and death. Just the contrary – on the straightforward, physical level he laid it on with a trowel. He simply gave it to you perfectly straight. Raggylug and the snake, Molly Cottontail going through the ice, Hekla and the Silver Fox drifting down to death on the ice floes, the nest-building sparrow who accidentally hanged himself in a length of horsehair, the murder (for that is what it amounted to) of Krag, the Kootenay Ram – I have never forgotten these and similar incidents in Seton's work. They were honest and true, as the horrors in Conan Doyle's *Brigadier Gérard* or R. M. Ballantyne's *Coral Island* were not. (Those seem, in several cases, the nasty, crypto-masturbatory offshoots of repressed minds – and that, too, I sensed instinctively at an early age.) If the physical truth is cruel and terrible, be a man and say so (but don't be a pervert and say so), and you may help your reader more than you know. This idea underlies the crushed hedgehog on the road in *Watership Down*, Bigwig in the snare and the gassing of the Sandleford warren recounted by Holly. (Should Bigwig have died after fighting Woundwort? Perhaps he should. I return to this below.)

The first 'great' book which I encountered with no holds barred was *The Pilgrim's Progress*, and I had the good luck to encounter it all by my-self, without any intermediary, at a relatively early age – seven. The gardener was a devout 'chapel' man and he simply lent it to me as he might have lent it to anyone; in a little, square, dark-green, cloth-bound edition with tiny, but perfectly clear, marginal steel engravings; which you could treat fairly roughly because it was rather worn already and anyway the gardener wouldn't be particular about a book as, say, your godfather would. I felt a tremendous respect for the book (and perhaps for myself for reading it?) I read it stolidly, with all the disputes and doctrinal conversations, which I was quite incapable of understanding. Nevertheless, those conversations did something for me. Unconsciously, I realized that parenthesis has a valuable part to play in a relatively long book (at that age it seemed to me a relatively long book) by giving the reader a rest and by making divisions between 'peaks' – dramatic, objective adventures which would otherwise crowd each other. (Later, of course, I came across the same technique in *Pickwick Papers*.) I had little idea what Christian and Co. were disputing about, but I knew it must be something valuable, or the book wouldn't still be there after two hundred and sixty years, or whatever it was. I remembered this when deciding to include, in a book which was going to be long anyway, the parenthetical tales of El-ahrairah and the two narratives of Holly. Simply that the immediacy of the main action is taken away for a time, gives the reader a respite – which is what I got from Mr Bunyan's incomprehensible doctrinal conversations. (Well, you wouldn't want Giant Despair following immediately upon poor Faithful's death in Vanity Fair, would you? The reader couldn't possibly respond properly.)

At that date you could not escape the Pooh books – you were rolled in them by the grownups, who loved them. So did I, and I am ready to defend them now. There is, of course, a lot wrong with them. The stories are so slight as not to be stories at all. They insult the reader's dignity, really, by *babying* him. ('Could you very sweetly – ?') The humour is often arch and falsely precocious. There is a cloying sentimentality in places. But one thing the Pooh stories have, pressed down and running over. They have marvellous characters; clear, consistent, interacting upon each other, each talking like himself – as good as Jane Austen's, in their own way. The relationship of Pooh and Piglet is splendid. Tigger is unforgettable. So is Eeyore – as far as I know, the first portrait in English literature of a type of neurotic we all know only too well; though perhaps he owes a little to Mrs Gummidge, 'the lone, lorn crittur' in *David Copperfield*. From the Pooh books I learned the vital importance, as protagonists, of a group of clearly-portrayed, contrasting but reciprocal characters –

though I wouldn't claim that Hazel, Fiver and Co, come anywhere near Pooh and his friends. It would take Tommy Handley, Colonel Chinstrap and Mrs Mopp to do that, though I'd also be prepared to admit Doctor Dolittle and his household.

But 'Journey', I can hear someone saying. Surely you derived from the Pilgrim's Progress the concept of Journey, didn't you? Perhaps I did – but here it is another book which I think of. No one told me about it. I had never heard of it. I found it by myself, in my prep. school library, at the age of eleven. It was a first edition (by Duckworth) and had at that time been extant only seventeen years – Walter de la Mare's *The Three Mulla-Mulgars* (now known for the worse as *The Three Royal Monkeys*). For me, this great work was a milestone of profound importance. It opened my eyes. A tear springs to my eye as I think of what I owe to it. At the time, it seemed that this alone was a story and that all others were mere attempts at stories. I need not speak of the Mulgars' journey. From it I understood, darkly, that we are all wandering in the snow, to an unknown destination beyond darkness and hypnotic water. Never pretend otherwise. I understood, too, for the first time, that the greatest achievement of a great novel is to create, by feeling, selection and emphasis, a particular world, having its own colours, its own sun and moon, climate, atmosphere and values (how inadequate are words), more real than those of the actual world, to which the devoted reader can return again and again for delight and comfort. Years later, I was able to meet Walter de la Mare and thank him – thank God. Once only have I ever experienced the same thing with comparable force and passion. Seven years afterwards, at Oxford, the music of Chopin hit me like a thunderbolt and became for many months a coloured lens through which all the world was seen.

To try to copy *The Three Mulla-Mulgars* would be like trying to copy *King Lear*. But involuntarily, certain specific incidents and features of *Watership Down* undoubtedly reflect, *mutatis mutandis*, that unparalleled work – rather as the William books may be said to reflect *Huckleberry Finn*. Most obviously, of course, there is the weakling hero with the second sight who guides and saves his friends, sometimes despite their disbelief or contempt. Fiver is Ummanodda, no danger. And Fiver's meeting, in a trance, with the man putting up the board in memory of Hazel, recalls Nod's dream of the Oomgar's spelling-book, which led him to save the Moona-Mulgar who had fallen over the ledge during the fight with the eagles. The Black Rabbit of Inlé owes something to the

Immanâla; though she is wicked and hateful, while the Black Rabbit is not. He is, rather, a counterpart of the Hindu Kali – the terrible but necessary death-aspect of God's face.

One thing of a different nature I owe to *The Three Mulla-Mulgars*. My family, all of them, scoffed and jeered – a shade harshly, I fancy – at my passion for it. No doubt I was a bore, but the pain taught me, once and for all, never to mock any child's feeling for any book – you never know what it may mean to him. And it drove the Mulgars underground, to germinate in silence and darkness – the best conditions for such a process, I dare say.

Early, too, I came upon the ghost stories of M. R. James and of Algernon Blackwood, for my elder sister introduced me to them when I was about ten. Oh boy, was I frightened by those ghost stories? I can remember lying in bed on a light summer evening, sweating with terror and muttering over and over '*A cause du sommeil et à cause des chats*' – surely a marvellously mysterious, minatory and disturbing phrase? In these stories I watched their writers building up tension by the use of little, vaguely-disturbing touches and incidents, and the worrying, harassing and baiting of the reader; the step-by-step technique; the use of some apparently innocuous phrase ('There *is* no kitchen cat') to turn the screw a little tighter and to lure the reader into frightening himself far more effectively than straight talk could ever frighten him. Then suddenly, the trap goes off. The awful figure of crumpled sheets sits up in the empty bed, and the devil-creature from Canon Alberic's scrapbook is crouching beside the reader's own chair. Undoubtedly, the mounting sense of unease and the feeling that something is wrong in Cowslip's warren owes something to M. R. James, even though the episode is not a supernatural one. Perhaps it is not entirely successful – one or two people have told me that they knew the answer before the trap went off (and Bigwig in it). Still, for the matter of that, one knows there's going to be a ghost – but precisely *how* will it appear and when, and what will it do? (All James's ghosts are malignant.) But the other passage of tension-building – Bigwig in Efrafa – is, I fancy, reasonably effective. A bit of appropriate weather can help a lot in bringing off the atmosphere of such an episode, but I can't trace the Efrafan thunderstorm to any book of my childhood. I think that that may owe most to the heat in Moscow in *Crime and Punishment*, and to Walter de la Mare's short story *Crewe*.

*Moonfleet* is a wonderful book (and has quotations as chapter-headings –

not very apt ones, for the most part, I fear – but a nice idea to borrow).
My brother used to take it back to boarding-school with him and re-read
it time after time. Nothing in it is more moving than the character of
Elzevir Block, the strong, grim man who never complains of his wrongs
and in the end gives his life to save the hero's. Actually, Elzevir hazards
his life for the hero twice before the end on Moonfleet beach – once on
the Zig-Zag and once at Carisbrooke well. I am sure that he contains the
germ of Bigwig, who survives the snare, fights the cats at Nuthanger
Farm and goes alone into Efrafa before he finally meets Woundwort in
single combat. To live up to Elzevir, Bigwig should have died in that
fight. It would have been right artistically, but I could not bring myself
to do it, or face up to depicting the grief of the other rabbits. Nor did I
really want to attempt that most difficult of feats, a muted, half-happy
ending. Besides, my daughters did not want Bigwig to die – and would
anyone else have preferred it, really? After all, the book is escapist fantasy.

Trying to be funny. There are really two different ways of trying to be
funny, or so it seems to me. The first is simply by making characters make
supposedly funny remarks, and the second is by devising intrinsically
comic situations. One employs both together, of course. For a model,
look no further than *Twelfth Night*. The second appears at first glance to
be the more difficult, but fortunately there are only about five basically
funny situations and they have all been used so often by the masters that
plagiarism is not just easy – it's unavoidable, so you might as well get on
with it. As to the first, very early on – almost as an infant – I learned the
value of having, in a straight story, one character who says (one hopes)
funny things. There is a book of about 1908 – I trust that many still read
it – called *Why-Why and Tom Cat*. (The author calls herself 'Brown
Linnet' and who she was I don't know.) Why-Why is a little girl who
learns about animals from her friend Tom-Cat (a kind of crypto-father
figure, really). The comic relief is provided by the Kitten-Cat, who goes
in for exchanges such as: 'It is my birthday.' 'You are too little to *have* a
birthday,' replied Tom-Cat, severely. 'But I mean it is *going* to be my
birthday,' said the Kitten-Cat. 'I shall be *one*!' Again, in the books about
Josephine and her dolls (girls' books, of course) dating from the time of
the First World War, there is a delightful character, a duck doll in a
sailor suit, called Quacky Jack. Quacky Jack is the naughty boy and keeps
up a running fire of bolshie remarks, some of which, when you are six or
seven, are killingly funny, and with us became family catch-words. (E.g.

When put under a sheet, 'for his good', to stop him anticipating a surprise in preparation – 'I don't care about my good – I want to see'.) Bluebell is not up to the standard of Quacky Jack or the Kitten-Cat, but he tries – and at least he sparked off, with his fooling, Blackberry's brain-wave with the punt. That was useful – how else to make it convincing?

The El-ahrairah stories derive from folk-tales, of which any good nursery, of course, is full. We had Andrew Lang, naturally, but I also had a splendid book called *Stories of the Birds from Myth and Fable.* (Author's name forgotten.) I wish I had it now. (Could anyone help?) Only one of the El-ahrairah stories, however, was actually lifted from a real folk-tale – the one about Hufsa and the trial of El-ahrairah. In the Russian story, an old peasant finds a hoard of gold in the forest, but his wife is such an inveterate gossip that he dares not bring it home, or the whole village will get to know and the lord of the manor or the bailiff will have it off him. So when he and she go together to pick up the gold, he arranges in advance that their journey shall be full of fantastic incidents. E.g. he puts a pike up a tree. Later, she tells all the incidents to the village, with the result that no one believes a word about either the journey or the gold. All the other four El-ahrairah stories (one of which, of course, is not funny) are simply 'in the manner of'. Perhaps they have their prototypes, but if so I can't place them consciously. I think the Uncle Remus stories have some relevance, too, but no adventure of El-ahrairah is lifted from Brer Rabbit. What I do feel I owe to Joel Chandler Harris, however, is the meticulous care which he takes to render dialect in carefully-considered and accurate phonetics. Uncle Remus you can hear to perfection. Thus encouraged, I took a deal of pains over the speech of the farmhands and of Lucy and her father, and if they're not accurate Hampshire, then it can't be done, I reckon.

But Kipling unimitated, inimitable Kipling, how shall I describe thee? Beyond argument, no one has ever written books more full of enjoyment for children. *The Just-So Stories,* the Jungle Books, *Puck of Pook's Hill* and *Rewards and Fairies* have no equal; and while we are about it, I would like to include the Barrack-Room Ballads. I remember well a dormitory-full of twelve- and thirteen-year-olds laying aside their own books on a Saturday night to listen to one of us who felt impelled to read the ballads aloud, with passionate intensity. Eleven years later he was killed in Normandy, and I can never read 'Ford o' Kabul river in the dark' without remembering him. Re-assessing these books as an adult, and in the light of Kipling's work as a whole, it seems to me that he was, in a sense, at his happiest and best in writing them, for to a child audience his fault of sententious didacticism is not irritating as it is to adults, and in these tales his fault of a certain insensitivity and banality – even vulgarity – (so wittily caricatured by Max Beerbohm) seems to fall away from him. The stories are often, in fact, extremely sensitive, and possess a sure imaginative empathy. It is very hard to find any fault at all with the best of them – *The King's Ankus*, *Red Dog*, the Sir Richard Dalyngridge stories and *The Knife and the Naked Chalk*. Can I claim to have been influenced by them, in the sense that my work shares any of their qualities? No, in that sense I cannot. But nevertheless, in two very important respects Kipling has his finger firmly in the *Watership Down* pie, and without him those lines would never have been written – or certainly not in the way they are. First, Kipling's illusion-formula for an anthropomorphic fantasy is an excellent one – so I deliberately copied it. The point is interesting, at any rate to any carpenter of tales. How exactly do you go about an anthropomorphic fantasy? Beyond one end of the scale altogether – a sort of ultra-violet – stands Henry Williamson. *Tarka the Otter* is superb natural history, but for that very reason it is neither a novel nor an anthropomorphic fantasy; nor is it meant to be either. It is simply an account of the life and death of a real otter. Next comes Ernest Thompson Seton. He wrote about real animals living their lives, but he shaped the stories a shade beyond straight *tranche de vie*, and was not concerned positively to stress, as Williamson does, that an animal is not a human being. To read Seton, you'd think, often, that an animal *is* quite like a human being. At the extreme other end of the scale is Kenneth Grahame, whose animals are simply humans disguised in animals' bodies. All anthropomorphic fantasies have to pick a point along that line. The genre is an illusion-game. What's your particular formula? Kipling ensured retention of his animal protagonists' dignity (and also, I think, of their essential animal nature, albeit anthropomorphized), while leaving himself a very wide scope for his narrative powers. His rule is (and you need a rule to be bound by, to keep your invention within a disciplined and consistent frame) to attribute to his animal characters human thoughts, human powers of converse, even human values (e.g. loyalty) but never to make them do anything of which real animals would actually be physically incapable. I can't help feeling, with all due respect, that I may even have played a little fairer than Kipling in one way. His animals have some rather up-stage motives at times, based on the 'Law of the Jungle', etc., Hazel & Co., however, are never concerned with anything except food, survival and mating. Otherwise, like Baloo and Kaa, they certainly do things animals *wouldn't* do, but never anything they *couldn't* do.

The other Kipling influence can be simply stated. Don't be afraid to let your writing be difficult, or to make big demands on your readers. Say what you have to say and don't be deterred by wondering whether they're going to be able to follow you. I have been pleasantly staggered to receive letters of obviously sincere appreciation from eight-year-olds; I wouldn't have thought anyone under ten could tackle *Watership Down*. It only goes to show. Apparently straight writing carries some kind of readability of its own. But after all, eight-year-olds read the Authorized Version quite happily. When I began on Kipling, I was eleven. It seemed very difficult stuff then, but the difficulty was part of the fascination. No doubt he knew that.

I believe writing is rather like chess in the respect that although there are certain useful rules to bear in mind, a lot of these should really be torn up at discretion. As far as learning how to do it goes, there is no substitute for continually studying the games of the great players. As fast as you try to articulate rules for writing for children (or for anybody else), someone will triumphantly break them. What else did Lewis Carroll and Kenneth Grahame do? (Anyway, what are the rules about writing for adults – perhaps we ought to have a few of those too?) I would say, beware principles and rules about writing for children – the value of an established moral order and all that. One can easily get so blinkered by the rules that one can no longer judge a book by the light of the heart. That light, of course, is what is used by the children themselves – of whom the Lord, in one of His most enigmatic and dazzling utterances, said: 'In heaven their angels do always behold the face of my Father.' And we all want to do that, don't we?

# NOTES ON CONTRIBUTORS

RICHARD ADAMS First book published 1972. Author of *Watership Down* (Rex Collings); *Shardik* (Allen Lane). Carnegie Medal, 1972; *Guardian* Children's Fiction Award, 1973

JOAN AIKEN First book published 1953. Author of *The Wolves of Willoughby Chase*; *Black Hearts in Battersea*; *Night Birds of Nantucket*; *The Whispering Mountain*; *Midnight is a Place*; *A Harp of Fishbones* (all Cape). *Guardian* Children's Fiction Award, 1969; American Mystery Writers' Award, 1972

NINA BAWDEN First book published 1952. Author of *A Handful of Thieves*; *The Runaway Summer*; *Carrie's War* (all Gollancz); and, among her adult books, *Anna Apparent, A Woman of My Age* and *George Beneath a Paper Moon* (all Longmans). Runner-up for *Guardian* Children's Fiction Award, 1974

HELEN CRESSWELL First book published 1961. Author of *The Piemakers*; *The Signposters*; *The Nightwatchmen*; *The Outlanders*; *Beachcombers*; *The Bongleweed* (all Faber). Runner-up for Carnegie Medal, 1967, 1969, 1971, 1973

PENELOPE FARMER First book published 1960. Author of *The Summer Birds*; *Charlotte Sometimes*; *A Castle of Bone*; *William and Mary* (all Chatto & Windus)

NICHOLAS FISK First book published 1962. Author of *Space Hostages*; *Trillions*; *Grinny*; *High Way Home*; *The Bouncers*; *Emma Borrows a Cup of Sugar* (all Hamish Hamilton)

JANE GARDAM First book published 1971. Author of *A Few Fair Days*; *A Long Way from Verona*; *The Summer After the Funeral* (all Hamish Hamilton)

LEON GARFIELD First book published 1964. Author of *Jack Holborn*; *Devil-in-the-Fog*; *Smith*; *The Drummer Boy*; *The Strange Affair of Adelaide Harris*; *The Sound of Coaches* (all Kestrel, formerly Longman Young Books). *Guardian* Children's Fiction Award, 1966; Arts Council Award for the Best Book for Older Children, 1966–68; Carnegie Medal 1970 (with Edward Blishen)

JOHN GORDON First book published 1968. Author of *The Giant Under the Snow*; *The House on the Brink* (both Hutchinson)

RUSSELL HOBAN First book published 1958. Author of *The Sea-Thing Child* (Gollancz); *Bedtime for Frances*; *The Mouse and His Child* (both Faber); and, among his adult books, *The Lion of Boaz-Jachin and Jachin-Boaz* and *Kleinzeit* (both Cape). Whitbread Library Award for Children's Books, 1974 (with Jill Paton Walsh).

C. WALTER HODGES First book published 1939. Author of *The Namesake*; *The Marsh King*; *The Overland Launch*; *Shakespeare and the Players* (all Bell); *Shakespeare's Theatre* (Oxford). Kate Greenaway Medal, 1965

MOLLIE HUNTER First book published 1963. Author of *Patrick Kentigern Keenan*; *The Haunted Mountain*; *The Thirteenth Member*; *The Lothian Run*; *The Stronghold*; *A Sound of Chariots*. Children's Book Award of the Child Study Association of America, 1972; Scottish Arts Council Award, 1973

URSULA LE GUIN First book published 1964. Author of *The Wizard of Earthsea*; *The Tombs of Atuan*; *Farthest Shore* (all Gollancz); and, among her adult books, *Left Hand of Darkness, Lathe of Heaven* and *Dispossessed*. American National Book Award, and Newbery Silver Medal,

PHILIPPA PEARCE First book published 1954. Author of *Minnow on the Say*; *Tom's Midnight Garden* (both Oxford); *Mrs Cockle's Cat*; *A Dog So Small*; *The Children of the House* (with Brian Fairfax-Lucy); *What the Neighbours Did and other stories* (all Kestrel, formerly Longman Young Books). Carnegie Medal, 1958; American Spring Book Award, 1963

K. M. PEYTON First book published 1947. Author of *Flambards*; *The Edge of the Cloud*; *Flambards in Summer*; *Pennington's Seventeenth Summer*; *The Beethoven Medal*; *Pennington's Heir*; *A Pattern of Roses* (all Oxford). Carnegie Medal, 1969; *Guardian* Children's Fiction Award, 1969

IAN SERRAILLIER First book published 1944. Author of *They Raced for Treasure*; *Flight to Adventure*; *The Silver Sword* (all Cape); *The Ivory Horn* (Oxford); *The Midnight Thief* (BBC); *Marko's Wedding* (Deutsch). Junior Book Award, Boys' Clubs of America, 1960; runner-up for Carnegie Medal 1956, 1960

CATHERINE STORR First book published 1952. Author of *Marianne Dreams*; *Marianne and Mark*; *Robin* (all Faber)

ROSEMARY SUTCLIFF First book published 1950. Author of *The Eagle of the Ninth*; *The Lantern Bearers*; *Warrior Scarlet*; *The Mark of the Horse Lord*; *The Shield Ring*; *The Truce of the Games* (all Oxford). Carnegie Medal, 1959, and twice runner-up for Hans Christian Andersen Award, 1975

JOHN ROWE TOWNSEND First book published 1961. Author of *Gumble's Yard*; *Hell's Edge*; *Widdershins Crescent* (all Hutchinson); *The Intruder*; *Goodnight, Prof, Love*; *Forest of the Night* (all Oxford). PEN Silver Pen Award, 1970; *Boston Globe* – Horn Book Award for outstanding text, 1970; 'Edgar' awarded by Mystery Writers of America

GEOFFREY TREASE First book published 1934. Author of many novels, the latest being *Popinjay Stairs* (Macmillan). Also *This is Your Century*; *Tales Out of School*; and two volumes of autobiography, *A Whiff of Burnt Boats* and *Laughter at the Door* (Macmillan). *New York Herald Tribune* Award, 1966

JILL PATON WALSH First book published 1966. Author of *Hengest's Tale*; *The Dolphin Crossing*; *Wordhoard* (with Kevin Crossley-Holland); *Fireweed*; *Golden-*

grove; *The Emperor's Winding Sheet* (all Macmillan). American Spring Book Award, 1970; Whitbread Library Award for Children's Books, 1974 (with Russell Hoban)

BARBARA WILLARD First book published 1958. Author of *The Battle of Wednesday Week; The Lark and the Laurel; The Sprig of Broom; A Cold Wind Blowing; The Iron Lily; Harrow and Harvest* (all Kestrel, formerly Longman Young Books). *Guardian* Children's Fiction Award, 1974